Ozana Giusca

SHORTCUT TO BUSINESS SUCCESS

101 Zero-Cost Tactics to Take Your Company to the Next Level

Amaze Yourself With What YOU Can Achieve Further!

ISBN-13: 978-1499790375
ISBN-10: 1499790376

To all the business owners and entrepreneurs I have worked with: thank you for entrusting me with growing your business.

To my team, who have put so much effort into building our Tooliers® business tools as well as helping me with this book: thank you! Another big thank you to my consulting team, whom I can totally rely on to provide the best service to our clients. None of this would have been possible without you!

Table of Contents

Foreword

The world is changing so fast. These events are opportunities for those who grab them, and at the same time can negatively affect others who do not take action. Most small businesses find it harder to break through their current level. They reach a plateau and do not know what step to take next, or go beyond 'small' and lose the plot.

There is so much information available now about how to run a successful business, but the challenge is to find meaning within this information and to use it appropriately to optimize and grow one's business. In my experience as a small business consultant, I have seen a lot of business owners who cannot simply and quickly explain what they do, let alone generate interest and sell their products or services. I also discover that entrepreneurs have dreams, goals, but 80% of their time is spent on things that have no link whatsoever with their objectives. If they do not focus on what is needed to achieve their goals, how can they get there?

If you are looking for a very hands-on approach to building your business from the ground up, Ozana has nailed it in *Shortcut to Business Success.* What a purposeful read for anyone who is an entrepreneur or small business owner. As you continue on your business or career journey, you will face real challenges that may deter you from achieving your biggest goals. The tactics in this book will keep you on track and help you reach your goals in record time.

In our lives we have the opportunity to do it the hard way or to learn from what the experts do, and then do it better. Ozana has been trained by some of the best in the business, including business and marketing guru Jay Abraham. In this new book you will discover key observations and ingredients to create even more success in your life and business. The real-world examples, as well as the practical exercises at the end of each chapter, also ensure this is a user-friendly manual to reaching business success.

In *Shortcut to Business Success*, you will learn to see the bigger picture of your business as well as discover the importance of *systematically* improving it; that is, by prioritizing and focusing on those areas that most need improvement. You will learn to identify your best customers; let go of any customers who do not lift your business; learn from your competitors; and fulfil the core purpose of every business: providing *real value* to your customers. You will also discover how creating the right kind of partnerships will grow your business with little

extra effort on your part. Business owners will find the tactics on closing sales and creating urgency especially valuable. You will also see how essential it is to build relationships both with your best customers and your team.

This book is also brutally honest about areas in which business owners tend to waste time and resources – and provides a wealth of best practices for time management; this includes a reminder to employ the time-saving advantages of certain technologies. You will also be encouraged to reflect and act upon your role as a leader and to go beyond merely managing your business to making sure it leads to the kind of life and lifestyle you desire. Aspects like personal branding, networking and being open to change are also discussed. Finally, you will clarify your vision in order to take your brand into the future and be left with a business that is dynamic and that constantly strives for – and achieves – improvement and growth.

The bottom line: if you are ready to increase your success rate today, take the time to read this mind-expanding book two to three times, and then implement the ideas that are shared here.

Bill Walsh

America's Small Business Expert

Preface

If you answer YES! to any of these statements, this book is for you.

- You have achieved some success with your business, but seem unable to grow it further.
- You are not satisfied with where your business is.
- You are not getting enough from your business (you are not getting enough recognition or enough money, or you have not succeeded in fully achieving your Objectives).
- Work is taking over your life and you have no time for family, relaxation, or travel.
- You are still struggling to make a living.
- You are bored with your work! You want something more challenging and fun.
- You are missing something, but you're not sure exactly what.
- There are some areas you do not understand (for example, finance) or you are passionate about your product, but you cannot sell it.
- You just want to be sure that you are on top of things and that your business is on the right track.
- You have some ideas for new businesses, but are not quite sure how to go about it.
- You want new challenges, but you need your current business to continue to run for various reasons (financial, community).
- Your turnover and/or profits have started decreasing.
- You can anticipate a disaster but you cannot tell what exactly is happening.
- Your best employees have started to leave.
- You have lost your biggest client.
- You seem to deliver good quality but your clients are still not prepared to pay what you'd like for your products.
- There has been a recent change in your company's industry or outside environment and this has had a great impact on your business.
- You and your staff are working too hard and it is just not fair on any of you (especially given the results you achieve).
- You consider your company a victim of your crisis, a system, or something else.

- Your business has stopped serving the community.
- Your business is growing quickly and you are struggling to manage it. It is becoming too complex for you to run on your own.
- Your life is too stressful. There are just too many problems that need to be solved by you, the business owner.
- You and your co-owners have trouble running the business together.
- Your business has started experiencing problems or you foresee problems, but you don't know what to do.
- You have accumulated too much debt in your company and can no longer sustain it.
- You simply want to discover the latest strategies that Fortune 500 companies use for their success!

My Story

Hello, Ozana Giusca here. I want to take a few minutes to ask you the questions that are on every small business owner's mind…

- Can I REALLY make much more money yet work less?
- What is the REAL secret behind those businesses that generate more profits while their owners are enjoying life and doing what they want, when they want?
- Can I get more customers even with such a small team already maxed out?
- Can I get better and bigger customers, even if I don't know how to market, or even if I do everything possible already for my business? Can I get more customers to call us instead of us chasing them?

I get asked these questions all the time… and that is why I wrote this book. *Shortcut to Business Success* contains the answers to all these questions, and many more.

But before you dig in, let me tell you a little about myself.

After attaining my MBA from Cass Business School, London in 2000, I worked in the City for a few years. In 2003 I set up my own consulting firm. I managed to sell a few companies, raise hundreds of millions in bank finance for our clients, and I made a decent income. I increased my team to 10 consultants, I bought a flat, then another one, then the office for our company, a new car, took holidays around the world… I was a rising star, doing everything that most would love to do…

Until late 2007, when the crisis hit my business *badly*. All of a sudden money stopped flowing in. The banks withdrew from financing our transactions; those hundreds of thousands of dollars in success fees never arrived; and ongoing consulting projects got put on hold. No more new business meant no more cash.

I had to let most of my team go. I felt terrible losing my consultants. For me, they were *family,* not just staff. And they were damn good at what they did.

With more than a million dollars in debt, I could not pay the bank anymore. Many sleepless nights followed… I felt ashamed, convinced that people would point their finger at me, accusing me of not paying my debts. I got scared thinking about a potential bad credit rating and that I would never again be able to get a loan.

I had no money coming in, and I had to borrow money to pay the two employees I was left with. I was driving to my father every weekend to get food for the week for my boyfriend and me.

Every phone call I got, every email I received brought bad news.

I even had my phone services provider threatening to cease their service should I not pay my bills. Imagine trying to save a business without a phone connection or access to the internet!

That was it, I decided. Enough! I borrowed more money and paid for an intensive four-day Business Mastery program presented by business mastery like Tony Robbins, Chet Holmes and Jay Abraham – as much as my whole MBA! A program that teaches business owners how to have Breakthroughs in business. A program that uses the same Strategies and Best Practices of the most successful businesses.

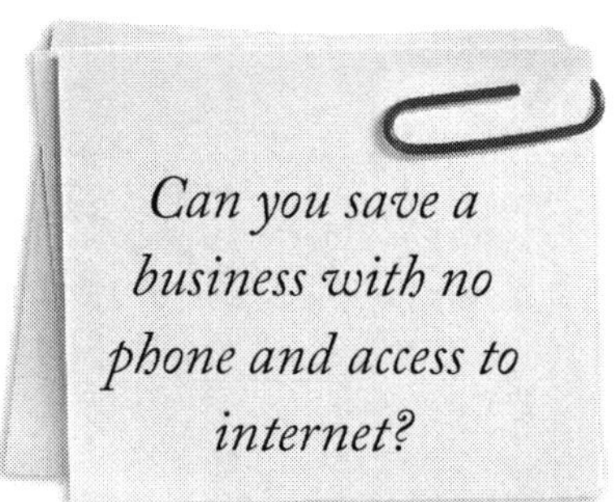

When I signed up, I received a big box of 32 DVDs, containing these strategies. I watched every evening, with pen and paper in hand. I took notes on the many great ideas to grow my business, but I still could not implement them as I had no time, no support team, no money.

During the live event, Tony Robbins presented some of these great strategies. If you don't already know him, Tony is the guru who makes possible the impossible. At some point, he asked, 'Who of you can't see yourself using what we have taught you here?' I raised my hand and he selected me. He must have seen the desperation in my eyes. My job was to convince Tony I was in an impossible situation. Within minutes he had made me realize that anything is possible. I was so empowered and became convinced I could take my business to the next level, that no one could stop me now.

Right after the course I started implementing some of the strategies and I could see results right away. Within three months I had $50,000 in my bank account, followed by $100,000 the next month, $200,000 the next month, and further exponential growth.

One day I got a call from Paul, who runs one of the most successful

international consulting companies. I think highly of him. 'Ozana, I see your business is flourishing, and I am amazed how you've managed to turn it around in such a short period of time. More so, to achieve such huge growth! What are you doing?'

'I watched various successful entrepreneurs; then I learned and adapted their techniques to my business,' I said.

'I have also been to such seminars,' replied Paul, 'and I've got access to this knowledge, but my business has not been growing, let alone at double digits in a month!'

Hmmmm.... Maybe THIS is my key to success. My ability to adapt and apply business best practices to any business. And to find a way to implement them in a simple manner and get rapid results.

> *What if there was a better way to achieve those dreams you had when you started your business?*

This is how I got the idea to put all that information – and much more – into what is today the **Business Lens™**, a toolkit to identify what you don't do well or enough of in your business. **This is a tool that reveals the naked truth about your business.** It measures, mathematically, the gap between the company being diagnosed and Best Practices. The bigger the gap, the more growth potential the company has.

In the past three years, I have personally helped more than 100 companies achieve massive growth. Some companies increased Sales by 30% within the first month of working with us; others tripled their Sales within a year. Pretty good, eh, given that they do not invest any money in this growth, and they don't have to work longer hours? In fact they work less, so they get to spend more time with their families and do what they love outside of work.

The economy changes rapidly these days. As a small business owner, it is easy to run your business as if lost in a dark forest, thinking only of survival. You might forget about the destination. You are most likely involved with paying the next bill, dealing with crisis after the best employee has left, trying to make up for that lost customer, deciding what kind of paper to buy for the copy machine and many other activities that keep you 'busy' and working hard. But do you work *smart*? What if there was a better way to achieve those dreams you had when you started your business?

One third of business owners **want to grow their businesses, but don't know how and where to start.** The rest would like to maintain their business. The reality, however, is that 80% of businesses fail in the first five years and 96% in the first 10 years (this according to Michael Gerber, author of *The E-Myth*).

This fact inspired me to write this book. I want to help you, a business owner, enjoy your entrepreneurship. I want to help small business owners like you really achieve the success they deserve.

This book is a collection of Best Practices I have seen and learnt about during my 18-year career in professional services. I learnt about these tactics from seminars, workshops, conferences, summits, and I have tried and tested them on my business and on our clients. If you master the tactics that follow, you will be able to compete with multinational companies, with Fortune 500 companies, *as their equal*. Because you know what? They use exactly the same tactics you are about to read in this book.

As a business owner you want to grow your company as much as possible in the shortest period of time. You will find a lot of tactics in this book that you will be able to apply immediately to your business, and some that you have never heard or thought of. The best approach is to be open to all the tactics and to then choose those that best suit, or are most applicable to, your business. Your decision regarding which tactics to implement will also depend on your Objectives and the Stage your business is at.

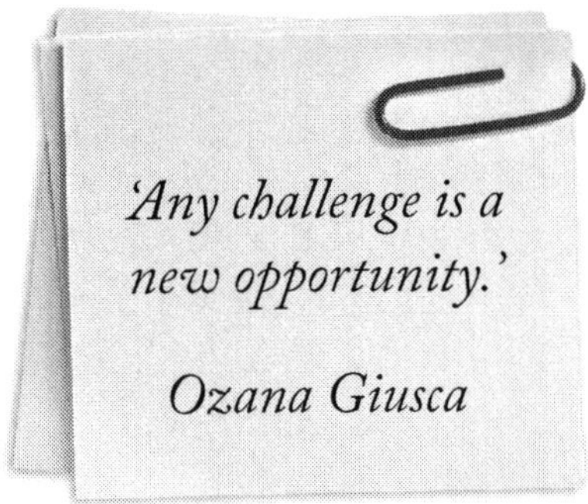

Introduction

How to use this book

You don't have to start with Chapter 1, or to read this book chronologically. Start with the chapter that feels the most interesting to you. Each chapter addresses a different Stage of a business. You may find one chapter more relevant than another. Read the relevant ones first and feel free to jump from one chapter to another.

You will see that each of the 101 Tactics concludes with a short exercise that will make it easy to apply the tactic to your business. If you are serious about growing your business, it is essential that you think about applying the tactic you have just read and *do the exercises* that follow. While doing the exercises, write down whatever comes to mind.

Don't get overwhelmed by all the information in this book. You don't have to use it all at once. However, you will be surprised by how much of this book applies to you and your business. Take the knowledge on board, and don't get desperate if you can't find a way of using it on the spot. The more you practice using these tactics, the more ideas you will get – in time you may even find ways to use those tactics you thought were not relevant to your business.

Revisit the book as your business Needs and Goals change. Reread certain chapters, or tackle new ones. This book may well become your 'Bible for business growth'.

The finer details

I switch randomly between female **(she/her)** and male **(he/him)** agents.

Definitions of all words or terms that appear in ***bold and italics*** can be found in the Glossary of Terms.

I use **customer** as a generic term. In your industry, you may prefer the word client, visitor, guest, user, or patient, for example.

I use examples from **a range of industries**. Feel free to use them to help you adapt and apply the tactics to your own business.

Throughout the book, I use **products** and **services** interchangeably. Note, however, that an **offering** is not the same as a product or service. For our purposes, an offering refers to the product or service combined with its price, packaging and positioning. So, product X as offering A is sold for $100 as a stand-alone product. Product X could also be packaged as offering B, which includes another item or addresses a different market or just has a different packaging, and sells for $200.

Introducing Tooliers®

Tooliers® (www.tooliers.com) is THE platform with business growth tools to offer small business owners all the instruments, tactics, knowledge and Best Practices that Fortune 500 companies use for their success, in a fun and affordable manner, so they compete with the largest companies in their industry, as their equals.

> ***For example:*** *Cashew nuts can be sold in large quantities (tons) to wholesalers, who then repackage the nuts in smaller quantities (say 1 kilogram) to be sold at the market. Those same cashew nuts can be sold in supermarkets in packs of 300 grams; these look more attractive and command a higher price. Or the cashew nuts can be sold per 100 grams in a high-end bar, for a premium price.*
>
> *The product is the same – cashew nuts – but with different packaging and/or positioning, it becomes a different offering and commands a different price.*
>
> *The target market could be the same or different. I could be buying a 1 kg pack at the market, but I could also buy the 300 gram packs in gas stations.*

Business Lens™ is the digital mirror of your business. It shows you the naked truth about your business. It shows your unrealized growth potential.

Business Lens™ Diagnosis is the process of using Business Lens™ to perform a full analysis of your business, which identifies the areas that need more of your attention so you take your business to the next level.

Business Doctor is one of our growth programs, where we perform the Business Lens™ Diagnosis, and issue suggestions and recommendations for tactics and strategies to execute, so you grow your business immediately as well as long term.

Businesses don't grow unless people grow. You rock! By reading this book, you are enabling personal growth together with business growth!

Chapter 1
Steady Growth - Systematize Your Business

Tactic #1

Follow a System

Focus your efforts exactly where they are required.

I have created the **6-S Focus Formula** (see below) because so often I see business owners focusing on the wrong things. You want to do what you like to do, or what you are best at and this is fine to a certain extent. But if you want to have a *highly successful business*, you need to approach it systematically, and change Focus according to which Stage your business is at. Focus doesn't mean you only work on a certain area of your business or that you do it all by yourself. It means you **concentrate your efforts on a particular area of your business at a particular time.** It also means that you learn more about that area. Of course, you can involve Experts and you can Delegate, as long as this area is where your mind is. Even if you outsource, you inevitably acquire more knowledge in that area.

Be disciplined and Focus on what you have to in order to reach your Objectives and fulfill your dreams.

6-S Focus Formula

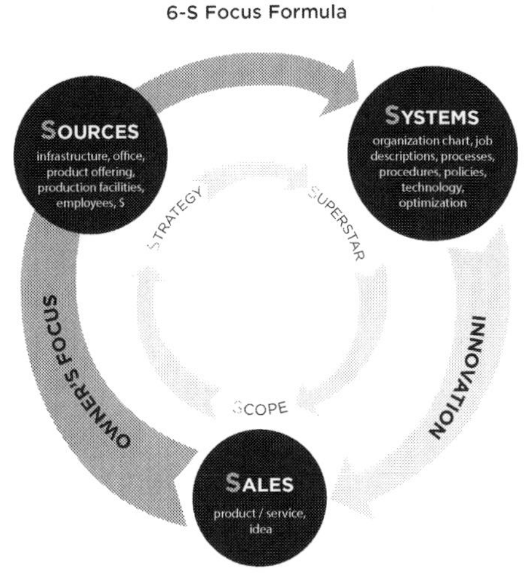

The idea is simple: your Focus, as the owner of the business, moves from 'Sales' to 'Sources and Resources' to 'Systems', as your company grows. This is the **best business growth strategy**. Focusing on one part of the business does not mean that you *only* deal with that part. It means, say, that you allocate half of your time to it, while the other half is split between anything else you would normally deal with. Above all, you, as the business owner, must focus on what needs your Focus, even if it is not necessarily what you *like* doing.

Let's talk about each area of a business:

1. Focus on Sales when you are at the beginning with your business, or when you launch a new product or open a new location. 'Sales' is split into two parts:

(i) selling your product or service;

(ii) selling your idea.

Selling your product or service is what you would generally understand as: giving your product / service to your customer in exchange for money (the price paid).

Selling your idea means getting people to buy into what you are doing. To share your dream, your vision and to get others excited about it. Selling your idea to current employees, potential employees, partners, suppliers, banks and any other person that is necessary to run the business smoothly, is as important as selling your product. You cannot create a business on your own. To achieve your Objectives, you need people around you. And those people don't join just because you think they should. It is tempting to believe they see and understand as you do, but they don't. You have to give them reasons to opt in, just as you give reasons to your customers to buy your product.

During this Stage, you have only a **Scope**. You know where you want to get to, but it is still vague. You need the market reaction and partners' Feedback in order to ensure you have the right product, the right offering, both for your *customers* and for your business partners. The offering for the customer is a widely used concept: 'Buy this product for this price because it solves this problem in this way.' The offer for *business partners* sounds something like this: 'Bring customers to our business and you get x% from all the money they spend with us.' This is how you have to think of the Value proposition for your customers and your business partners. All parties have to win. And everything has to make sense and be clear from the outset.

2. Focus on Sources and Resources once your product or service sells by itself; in other words, when customers buy your product or service without you having to convince each of them individually. By 'Sources' I mean everything that enables you to deliver to your customer; that is, your overall infrastructure: production facility, office space, logistics, as well as your employees and money to buy raw materials and invest in further growth. No point selling if you can't deliver, right?

3. When you have gotten to this phase, **you have a Strategy in place.** Now that you know what and how you sell, and for how much, you can create Specific Objectives and a clear path to achieving them.

4. Focus on Systems when you are confident that you have a product that sells and that you can deliver and satisfy your customer. By 'Systems', I mean organizational charts, job descriptions, processes, procedures, policies, IT system, and potentially CRM / ERP (software to help with planning and managing your Resources and your customers). In this phase you **consolidate what you have**; you organize things internally and clean up your mess. By this Stage, you and your staff have tried various ways of producing and delivering Value and you now know who does what in your company, and how. It is therefore time to document everything that is happening in your company, to put order in place. This helps you and your current employees to better understand how things are being done in your company and to become more efficient. Having these Systems in place also makes for an easier and more efficient process when you bring new people into your organization. You have 'machinery' that works, effectively and efficiently.

What you care about now is **becoming a Superstar Company**. By 'Superstar', I mean being the best in your niche. If you think of your industry as a pyramid, there is only one company on top, a few on the second layer, then the third, and so on... until the bottom, where you find plenty of companies. Your Objective is to **get as close as possible to the top**. Why? Because if anything destructive happens in the economy or in your industry, or if anything happens that can adversely affect your business, you hardly feel it if you are on top. The recent financial crisis resulted in so many companies going bankrupt or being close to bankrupt – this is because they were at the bottom of the pyramid in their niche. If a tsunami comes, or the state does construction on the road in front of your shop or office, you need to be in such a strong position that your business does not suffer. This is being a Superstar Company.

Shift Focus as your company develops and grows.

After Systems are in place, you need to focus on **Innovation** if you want to take your company to the next level, in which case you go back to Sales in another growth cycle. Alternatively, you retire or sell your company… or you leave it as is and continue to manage 'in the business', which will eventually go downhill.

The next question is 'When and how do I move from one area to another?'

TAKE ACTION NOW!

Based on the Stage of your business development, decide which of the three areas discussed above requires your Focus. Write it down:

____

____

____

What are your biggest current Challenges? Write these here; then use the tactics in this book to find ways of overcoming these Challenges.

Challenge 1:

____

Challenge 2:

____

Challenge 3:

____

Challenge 4:

____

Challenge 5:

____

Chapter 2
Attract More Customers

Tactic #2

Fire Your Worst Customers!

Remember the Pareto Principle: 80% of your results are produced with 20% of your effort.

Think about your current customers. Is it true that you prefer some to others? You might prefer some customers because they spend more money on your services, or because it doesn't cost you anything to acquire them, or because you easily serve them, or because your margins with them are higher. **The Best Customer is the ideal client**. Every business has preferred customers. By identifying the characteristics of your Best Customer, you can define and pursue a Strategy to attract them.

Do you have customers you wish you didn't have? If so, ditch them! Yes, get rid of those who moan and complain about your services, or who cost you too much to serve. You cannot (and should not) be everything to everyone.

Eighty percent of results are produced with 20% of your effort. If you focus your efforts on attracting the Best Customers, you may be surprised to see your Sales going up and your costs going down.

As a consultant, I get all sorts of business owners coming to me. On many occasions I have declined to work with them. You might ask, 'Who refuses business?' Well, smart people do. I refuse those clients that I anticipate will be difficult to deal with. I choose to work with those business owners that really want to put in the effort and do whatever it takes to grow their business. Their success is my success. I turn down those who do not seem committed, find excuses for not doing things, or question everything I tell them. I target those companies that have high ambitions. I give all my efforts to every client, but the results are that much better when a client is committed to learning and developing; these businesses grow significantly and much faster. Clients have to be open, willing and ready to put in the necessary manpower; if they are not, I take this as a sign that they are not really committed.

Think about it…
If you were a restaurant owner, would you rather have a local couple coming to your restaurant twice a week, bringing their friends and ordering the most expensive wine? Or would you prefer a group of students who orders the cheapest pizza and a soda and keeps your table occupied for three hours? You get to choose.

How do you choose your Ideal Client if you are a fashion logistics company? Your first answer might be that you are more than happy to work with any of these renowned fashion houses. It's such an honor for you! But if you take a closer look, you see that not all fashion businesses are the same. Zara changed the traditional cycle of fashion, involving two collections a year, with the breakthrough idea of bringing new designs to their shelves twice a week. As a reaction to Zara's success, about half of the famous fashion companies decided to make four to six collections yearly rather than two. You will have invested a lot of time and money to adapt to the fussy requirements of handling and transporting valuable fashion items. A good client for you is a fashion retailer that stocks very little and updates collections often because then you get to ship often. It seems a good idea to work with the companies that followed Zara's lead rather than the ones that are still changing their collections only twice a year.

TAKE ACTION NOW!

What are the characteristics of your Best Customers? Describe them in as much detail as possible, without giving names.

____

____

____

Name three of your Best Customers and state why for each:

1. ____
2. ____
3. ____

What are the characteristics of your Worst Customers? Describe them in as much detail as possible, without giving names.

____

____

____

Name three of your Worst Customers and state why for each:

1. ____
2. ____
3. ____

Tactic #3

Talk to the Final Decision-maker about Purchasing Your Product

Are you sure you are talking to the right person?

Determine who makes the final purchase decision and market your product or service to that person. **If you talk to the wrong person, you will find it almost impossible to sell anything** because this person doesn't have the final say. If you are selling copy machines to an office downtown, who is your customer? If the office manager, in this case, makes the buying decision, would you approach the CEO first or the office manager? Don't approach the CEO (or the PA) if the person with final say is the office manager!

Here's how it's done!
You sell plates and cutlery via retail stores. Who do you need to convince to buy your products? Think carefully... The retail chain's buyer? What happens if your products do not move from the shelf? Will that retail chain make follow-up orders from you? Of course not. So whom do you really need to talk to? The final customer! People like you and me, those who need your products. If we buy your products, the retail chain's buyer will order more.

Talk to both if you're not sure. This explains why time-share companies only invite couples for presentations. As they don't know which partner has the final say in the purchase decision, they want to have both present during the initial Sales presentation.

TAKE ACTION NOW!

Offering / product 1 (choose the offering or product you would like to work on and write it here):

____

Describe the Decision-maker, without giving names. Focus on characteristics.

____

____

____

Name the Decision-makers for three of your customers and explain why you have identified them as such:

1. ____
2. ____
3. ____

Offering / product 2 (choose the offering or product you want to work on and write it here):

____

Describe the Decision-maker, without giving names. Focus on characteristics.

____

____

____

Name the Decision-makers for three of your customers and explain why you have identified them as such:

1. ____
2. ____
3. ____

Offering / product 3 (choose the offering or product you want to work on and write it here):

____

Describe the Decision-maker, without giving names. Focus on characteristics.

____

____

____

Tactic #4

Provide the Best Value to Your Customer

Imagine, for a moment, that YOU are the customer.

Put yourself in your customer's shoes. (This is easier said than done.) Would *you* like to receive the service you provide? If the answer is no, you know what you need to do... if the answer is yes, ask yourself:

- How can I deliver an even better service?
- How can I provide the best service to this customer?

Think of those among your employees who interact with your customers: they are your Customer Satisfaction Team, not 'Customer Service'. It is easy to miss the subtle difference here. **Be sure you satisfy your customer, rather than just serve him.** Satisfy him completely and he will be pleased to do business with you again. A Happy Customer is a repeat customer and will also be more than happy to recommend you to friends or colleagues who may benefit from your product or service. This way, you sell more to existing customers and attract more Best Customers.

Be sure you satisfy your customer, rather than just serve him.

What will an unhappy customer do, other than not do business with you again? He will be on Facebook, posting about the unpleasant experience to his friends.

This is what we like to see!
Learn from Zappos founder and CEO Tony Hsieh. He started from a simple but somewhat novel idea – to sell shoes via the internet – and hit $1 billion in annual Sales in 2008. Zappos was so successful that Amazon acquired it at the end of 2009 for a reported $1.2 billion. The secret of this success was the company's obsessive dedication to taking customer service to new heights: their Organizational Culture championed the idea of constantly delivering a

'wow' experience to their customers. The Strategy was simple. In Tony's words: 'Our philosophy has been to take most of the money we would have spent on paid advertising and invest it into customer service and customer experience instead, letting our customers do the marketing for us through word of mouth.' (Tony Hsieh, Delivering Happiness: A Path to Profits, Passion, and Purpose).

TAKE ACTION NOW!

Offering / product 1 (choose the offering or product you would like to work on and write it here):

____

How can I deliver an even better service associated with this product?

____

____

____

How can I provide the Best Service to the customer that buys this offering?

____

____

____

Offering / product 2 (choose the offering or product you would like to work on and write it here):

____

How can I deliver an even better service associated with this product?

____

____

____

How can I provide the Best Service to the customer that buys this offering?

____

____

____

Offering / product 3 (choose the offering or product you would like to work on and write it here):

____

How can I deliver an even better service associated with this product?

____

____

____

How can I provide the Best Service to the customer that buys this offering?

____

____

____

Conclusion

How can I deliver an even better service in general?

____

____

____

How can I provide the Best Service possible to my customers in general?

____

____

____

Tactic #5

Ditch Flyers. Replace with Value Papers

Offer discount vouchers or free coupons to potential customers.

Replace flyers with ***Value Papers***. Value Papers are flyers that tell potential customers about the product, but also give them something for free or, at the very least, a discount. Value Papers have a *monetary* value for the holder with regard to the product on offer.

Think about it: when someone hands you a flyer while you are walking downtown, what do you do? You look for the first bin. Most people do. However, if you see some Value on that flyer, you think twice, right? You may want to use it or give it to a friend who could benefit from this offer.

Here's how it's done!
As a hotel owner you might ask the receptionist to give a voucher for a free 10-minute massage in your newly refurbished spa to all guests that check in. Would the person who tried your deep tissue massage not want more? I would!

If you are the manager of a Health Diagnostic Lab, instead of handing out flyers or displaying posters with your services start distributing vouchers for bonus cholesterol testing for those clients who sign up to have their risk for cardiovascular diseases tested. Turn your flyers into Value Papers by offering a free consultation to explain to clients what their test results really mean. Make the offer even more irresistible by providing a free consultation to help your clients design lifestyle changes and dietary plans aimed at reducing their specific health risks.

What if you're an agrochemical company selling fungicide to vegetable farmers? How could Value Papers work for you? You may say it's your retailer's business to convince farmers to buy your product – that's why they get a share of the pie. But think about this: you already spend a huge amount on those high-quality catalogues and brochures. It costs nothing more to use this tactic within the brochure you print. And instead of printing the classic flyers for your national and regional retailers to use at your next promotional conference, turn them into vouchers. This saves the retailer a lot of time and effort in convincing the farmer to buy from him, and gives farmers a reason not to bin that piece of paper. This is a simple way to help your retailer with zero extra costs. He gets better support from you and wins more Sales, which is good for you too.

TAKE ACTION NOW!

Create a discount offering (percentage discount) on your product. Write down the exact text you will print on the discount voucher.

____

____

____

Create a Voucher Offering (free gift) for your product. Write down the exact text you will print on the Gift Voucher.

____

____

____

Tactic #6

Study Your Competition

Learn from your Competitors. Copy and adapt to your business what works for them.

Firstly, identify your Competitors. Think of your Competitors as those companies that satisfy the same Need as you do, or tap into the same spending budget, within your target market. Satisfying the same Need doesn't mean selling exactly the same product. Think from the customer's point of view: it is summer, it is hot outside, and she wants something to cool her down. She may buy an ice cream or a soda. The ice cream and the soda are competing products in this case. By tapping into the same budget, think of a family that has a disposable amount of $2,000. They may choose to spend it on a holiday or on replacing the couch in their living room. Thus, the holiday and the couch become competing products.

If you think this way, you expand your horizon and may come up with ideas you would not have considered before. **Once you have identified your broad Competitors, select those whom it makes sense for you to study in more detail.** Research their company size, company structure, product portfolio, sales department actions, promotional actions and marketing budget, and the promotional channels they use.

Keep an eye open, study your Competitors and constantly look for ways to adapt their good ideas and take them to the next level, in your unique way.

Why study your Competitors? Think back to college: you like a girl and have asked her on a date, but another guy steals her from you. Do you not want to know why? Would you not ask around to learn more about the guy and try to understand why she prefers him? The same applies to business: you need to know *why* your clients choose your Competitors – so you change, you do something else, and next time they prefer *you*.

Here's another reason why you need to study your Competitors: to 'borrow' their ideas. If you see them doing something that works, why not do the same?

Back to college: if your roommate attracts all the boys' attention due to her pink shoes, wouldn't you buy a pair too?

Even if you are the best in your business and even if you believe your Competition should learn from you rather than the other way around, bear in mind that it's always a bad idea to underestimate your rival. Go visit their Facebook page – you will find great inspiration for your next social media campaign. Review their website too – you will get at least five tips to improve your own. You don't even need to find things you like on your Competitors' websites! **Becoming aware about what they do poorly might give you good ideas about how you could improve your own initiatives.** Businesses are complex structures and the environment continuously changes. It's almost impossible to be ahead on all lanes, all the time. Keep an eye open, study your Competitors and constantly look for ways to adapt their good ideas and take them to the next level.

Sign up to your competitors' newsletters so you get information on what they are doing and borrow some of their ideas.

Of course, in the real world, things are more complicated. You may need to use market research data to gain a proper understanding of your Competitors. For example, you may want to know the overall size of the market you operate in. Study how the size of your market has changed over the past five years, and how your customers' behavior has changed, and what influenced that change. Know the number of people employed in your industry and how this number has changed over the past five years.

Now we're talking!
I constantly look at people that are smarter than me (be they my Competitors or not), and try to apply what they do to my business. Of course, I adjust it appropriately. Recently I learned that Google does not ask their employees to work a certain number of hours per day; they do not even care how many holidays their employees take. What they care about is results. I have since implemented this in my company, and I notice my staff is more committed. Clearly I don't compare myself to Google, but that doesn't mean I cannot learn from them.

Let's say you are consulting company specialized in helping businesses improve their customer service experience. How can you integrate the business know-how of your Competitors in your industry? It is true that in your line of business everyone is reluctant to share expertise since expertise is the main asset for a management consultancy. You don't have to necessarily look for a new consulting methodology. Start with the things that are already out there in the open. How do they present their services on their website? What benefits do they promise to their potential client? Do they also offer Complementary Services such as Training or do they only offer consulting? Their approach could help you improve your own business model or at least optimize the way you promote your services. Have a checklist before you start looking for ideas from your Competitors. Start with things that are not that good in your business today. Remember, the Objective is to find ways to improve your business, not to convince yourself you are already better than your Competition!

TAKE ACTION NOW!

Offering / product (choose the offering or product you would like to work on and write it here):

____

List 3 Competitors offering this type of product:
1. ____
2. ____
3. ____

List 3 Competitors offering products within the same budget; i.e. what else would your target customer use the money for?
1. ____
2. ____
3. ____

List 3 alternative Solutions to the same problem you solve; i.e. how else can your target customer solve her problem? With which other types of products or services?
1. ____
2. ____
3. ____

You now have 9 competing offerings. Study them and gather ideas from each of them to implement in your own business. At the very least sign up to the Competitors' newsletters!
Then repeat this entire exercise on your other offerings or products.

Tactic #7

Educate Your (Potential) Customers…

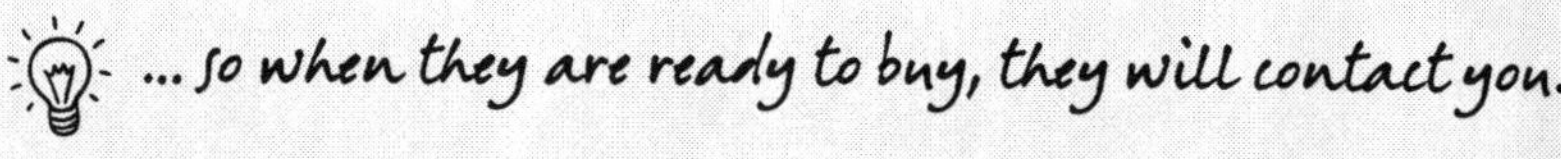

You may have excellent products and services, but people are tired of promotional messages. How can you still let the world know about your exceptional offering? Educational Marketing is one of the most effective ways to reach this tough audience. The idea behind ***Educational Marketing*** is quite simple: say something useful (i.e. informative) to your listener and she will open up and start paying attention to what you have to offer. Educate ***prospects*** so they buy from you when they are ready and inform others.

With Educational Marketing, you publish education-based materials (in all forms of media you use to communicate with your prospects) rather than focusing solely on publicity or 'buy my product' messages. For example, when you go to a trade show, your approach would be: 'Okay, you have this problem and you can solve it this way. And by the way, my product does XYZ.'

Apply this tactic to your business!

As a partner in a law firm, you could publish articles in which you present cases you have handled, what happened and why, and also what could have happened had the parties acted differently. This is interesting and educational for your audience, while you are seen as an Expert in your field and the person to go to when people need legal advice. (And of course, this Strategy reminds people that itperson to go to when people need legal advice. (And of course, this hy and end up in a disaster.) You might even raise awareness in your community about a front-page social problem and get involved pro bono in solving it. Constantly running social responsibility programs along this line would not only give everybody in the community a positive feeling about your brand, but also make your employees feel good about themselves and their firm.

Let's say you are a provider of heat pump systems for residential buildings. Your Objective is to show to real estate developers and managers the advantages of your sustainable technology in an educational and convincing manner. Don't only talk about the extra comfort and the lower costs in the long run for the home

owners who use your Solution. Explain how heat pumps consume less energy than traditional heating systems and contribute to lowering CO2 emissions. Explain how pump systems are safer because they work without oil, gas or other hazardous substances. This type of information can convince developers and give them support to sell the idea to their clients, the home buyers. You could say that running such a campaign is more expensive than simple promotion. That's not quite true. An important advantage of Educational Marketing (as opposed to traditional Sales-oriented Marketing) is that it has public relevance. Educational Marketing does not only educate the direct client (developers, building administrator), but also the final consumer (families buying the houses), the market, and society as a whole. This is helpful for you because it allows you to share the marketing costs. For example, strike a Partnership with an Association of real estate developers to include your technology in a larger campaign aimed at promoting sustainable technologies for residential buildings.

If you are a fashion retailer, teach your shop assistants to help their customers find the best clothes for their body shapes. Isn't it impressive to enter a shop, tell the shop assistant you want a jacket and learn immediately which is the best fit for you? Now that your assistants can teach the buyers about cut and size, you can get even more educative. Turn your vendors into beauty advisers for your clients, teaching them about the best colors for each skin tone. Apply the same strategy to sunglasses. Someone might find it hard to gauge which shape is best for her particularly round face. Instruct your assistants to share their Knowledge so that, next time, the customer knows on her own which models are worth trying on. Go one step further and tell the round-faced girl what would match her boyfriend's oval face. This makes her return to your shop every time she or any of her friends need another pair of sunglasses.

Educational Marketing also enables you to inform your customers in a way that bolsters your brand and the perception of its quality. For example, if you run a restaurant, you could incorporate educational content in your menu. Stun your guests with the premium ingredients you use in your salad, the special qualities of the sesame oil in your seafood or the fascinating history of your finest wine. Once impressed, your guests are more likely to happily pay the price for more expensive products.

Education-based messages:

- increase the power of your brand in the eyes of your customers, potential customers, or people who can recommend your offering;
- build top-of-mind awareness (when people want to buy what you offer,

they will immediately think of you / your company);

- help you and your business become an authority in your field – so you become the preferred choice without people ever questioning why;
- attract more clients, as well as enthused fans (who buy from you and recommend you to others).

Use any communication channel you can, such as mailings, newsletters, regular client surveys, public relations (PR), trade shows, awards ceremonies, industry seminars for the benefit of your clients, trade associations and internet.

TAKE ACTION NOW!

Write down 3 educational themes you could use to inform your audience about the Solution you provide and about your product / offering; i.e. what will you be talking about?

1.

2.

3.

Tactic #8

Use Joined Offers

Identify products that are already popular with the customers you want and add your product in a common offering.

Joined Offer refers to the promotion of your products together with the products of another business as a package or prize. With Joined Offers you have a larger reach for your dollar spent. In other words, **you capitalize on your partner's marketing budget, and your partner capitalizes on yours**. Your partner's customers get to hear about your product, and your customers get to hear about your partner's products. This is a win-win situation as both parties get more exposure.

Attention though! You want to associate your product with products of the same caliber. So, if you sell high-end shoes, you want to associate with high-end jewelry, and not with pizza, which is a low priced product. You need to think of products serving the same type of customer, or jointly solving the same problem for that customer.

They've put it into practice!

The Romanian government has introduced a rule whereby all companies have to facilitate employee health and safety training once a year. The accounting company we use put forward a particular company to do this training for us. We, like many of their clients, said yes; we needed the service and trusted their recommendation. The accounting company and the training company have developed a Joined Offer: when the accountants market their services to new clients, they always offer this training, which is done by the partner company. Together they satisfy the Need of their customers to comply with legislation: accounting for submitting the annual results of the company, and health and safety training of their employees. Of course, the partner company markets training together with accounting services to their ***prospects****.*

Some quick examples for you:

- Buy one pair of sneakers; get one slice of pizza for free.
- Buy one washing machine; get one bag of washing powder for free or at a discount.

- All-in-one salad: the salad producer makes a Joined Offer with the dressing producer, to offer the entire dish to the customer.
- Packaged holidays: particular flights, transportation and hotels are all included in the deal. All parties involved (the airline company, the hotel operator and the car rental agency) can promote this package to their customer base. Moreover, when the travel agent promotes this package, with one marketing budget (i.e. same dollar spent), it promotes products from three separate businesses.
- Let's go a little further. As a limo company you get your product (limousine hire) included in the offering. You would not promote this holiday package, but you would clearly benefit if the travel agent sells the package to a corporate client that treats its executives to a special weekend away.

TAKE ACTION NOW!

Write down the product for which you want to create Joined Offers:

____

Write down 3 types of products you could bring in to create a Joined Offer. In establishing Partnerships, consider the following: Which companies sell a ***Complementary Product*** to your target market? Alternatively, could you offer a full package or service to solve a series of problems for your customer in one shot?

1. Product for Joined Offer: ______________________
Jointly targeted customer: ______________________
Problem solved: ______________________

2. Product for Joined Offer: ______________________
Jointly targeted customer: ______________________
Problem solved: ______________________

3. Product for Joined Offer: ______________________
Jointly targeted customer: ______________________
Problem solved: ______________________

Tactic #9

Make Your Customer Feel Special

Use Personalized and Exclusive Offers or Gifts to make your customer feel she is 'the one'.

Do you like receiving compliments? Do you like to feel special? Do you like it when you are treated well? Of course you do. Why not do the same for your customers? Make them feel important – because they are important to you. Without them your business wouldn't exist! **Make them feel they are part of something Exclusive, so that they fall in love with your business.** By making your customers feel special, you also increase their loyalty. They will like you more, and they will want to do more business with you. We know that it costs seven times more to acquire a customer than to keep one. So, returning customers and repeat business means more profits!

Exclusivity has another advantage: it helps spread the word about your business. Imagine that you receive an invite to be part of an Exclusive Network for business owners. Would you accept? Of course you would. And you will probably tell the business next door that you have just joined this Exclusive Network. Now he wants to join too! You have just created more 'attraction' for this Network. Use this concept in your business to create your own 'Network' of Exclusive Customers.

Think of your first date with your loved one. How did you make her feel? How did she respond? You made her feel special, she was happy, and she agreed to see you again. And she would have told her friends how great you are!

This is what we like to see!

Zappos (see Tactic #4 'Provide the Best Value to Your Customer' for more on the company) sends a new customer a 'secret' email after her first purchase inviting her to an Exclusive VIP Club that gives her free second-day shipping privileges on all future purchases. Do you think she orders from them again? Of course she does!

TAKE ACTION NOW!

Write down 3 ideas that would make your customer feel special:

1. ____
____
____

2. ____
____
____

3. ____
____
____

Tactic #10

Use Customer Feedback

Your customers are the best source of information to improve your offering.

Feedback is the easiest way to understand what your customers think about your product or service. Feedback helps you understand what your customers want your product to become, and how they would like your service to improve. Get Feedback from customers and apply it to improve your products and services. **Ask specific questions and seek specific answers.** Really listen to the answers as they are given, and use them to better satisfy your customers.

Keep close to your customers and they will keep close to you.

Make sure you have a System in place to collect the Feedback and process it. If you don't collect Feedback, you may see your customers leaving your business but never know why. Make sure you seek Feedback in a way that leads your customer to give it to you. Don't do as I do when I ask my partner, 'How do I look like in this dress, darling?' and expect him to say, 'Wonderful, my love.' Ask your customer to be honest and take that honesty on board, so you can make real improvements. Design a questionnaire with yes / no answers or ratings from 1 to 10, as well as open questions, so your customer can express exactly what he likes and dislikes about your product or service. And if you don't know how to construct a Customer Feedback questionnaire, look at any you have received and let these assist you.

And remember, Customer Feedback should come from existing customers, as well as potential customers who then decided not to purchase from you. The latter helps you understand why they chose someone else.

Here's why you need to do this!

My consulting firm performed a full Diagnosis on a company selling special windows for residential houses. The scope of the Diagnosis was to identify any growth potential the business was not exploiting. When I delivered the Diagnosis Report to the business owner and recommended he put in place a

Customer Feedback System, he raised an eyebrow. His business generally has one-off customers so he didn't see the need for Customer Feedback.

During our conversation, he complained that a sales director was stealing business from him. This person had his own side company and was quoting lower prices to the same clients. My client said to me: 'Ozana, how could I have stopped this sooner? How could I have known that my most trusted employee was stealing business from me?'

The answer was obvious: if he'd had a Customer Feedback System in place, he would have received the Feedback that he was too expensive – his offers would of course always be more expensive than those from the company belonging to his sales director. He would have realized someone was constantly submitting lower priced offers to the same clients, and he would have discovered the malpractice much sooner. He took a year to understand what was going on; with Customer Feedback he might have understood within three months or less.

TAKE ACTION NOW!

Write down 3 areas of your business for which you would like Customer Feedback (for example, your product, customer service, distribution, or post-sale interaction):

1. ______________________________
____
____

2. ______________________________
____
____

3. ______________________________
____
____

Write down 3 specific questions you want answers to (from your customers):

1. ______________________________
____
____

2. ______________________________
____
____

3. ______________________________
____
____

Tactic #11

Tell Stories to Sell

Your customers are the best source of information to improve your offering.

People buy to satisfy a Need. They do not buy a product for the sake of the product. People buy a product because they want the perceived benefits the product offers them. Show Value, not price. Price is an important component of an offering, but it is Value that triggers the emotion to buy it. The features of the product are good to know, but the benefits determine whether the customer buys it.

Facts tell, Stories sell. Imagine when you were young that your parents had told you: the dragon is strong, blows fire through his mouth and eats people. Would you have been interested? Of course not. This is why they read the Story, from which you inferred all of the above.

In business, use Stories to demonstrate how existing customers have benefited from your product. Stories can help your ***prospects*** get to know you and trust you. The right Stories avoid confusion by expressing things in simple terms with which people are familiar. Stories also create curiosity. You seduce, slowly lifting the veil to reveal all of the delicious pleasures your product makes possible, or the pains it relieves. Stories can bypass skepticism and neutralize Sales resistance. You deal with objections within the Story. You also differentiate yourself from your Competition. Stories allow your potential customer to experience ownership of your product or service at that moment. And when they imagine not having your product, they feel upset or frustrated, and their desire for your product or service grows. Stories are personal, because the listener can build the picture in his own mind; he can 'see' it. At the end of the day, Stories are human!

Throughout this book, I tell you Stories of my life as a consultant. These Stories are used to illustrate a point, but they also position me as the Expert in my field. Do I tell you in this book how clever I am? No. Have you inferred that I am clever and that I can bring Value to your business? I hope so! I show you the Value I can bring to your business via examples (Stories), rather than by telling you: 'Hi, I am Ozana. I am the small business Expert who will help you massively grow your business.' Through Stories, I show you how I have helped other businesses, and you (hopefully) realize I can help your business too.

Recall a well-known TV advert for washing powder: after a soccer game, a boy's white T-shirt is covered in mud. His mother is happy after she washes the T-shirt with Brand X and it is once again impeccably white. To make the Story more interesting, you then see the T-shirt being washed with a different washing power – and it is not quite as white. From this Story you understand that Brand X is superior at keeping white clothes white. So Brand X becomes the obvious choice of washing powder. Through Story, the ad shows you the Value of using Brand X. It doesn't tell you which chemicals remove the dirt. It doesn't even tell you how much the product costs! The point of the Story is to make you want to buy Brand X only.

Of course, all becomes confusing when Brand Y shows you a similar Story, in which it is the washing powder of choice! This is why it is so important that your Story distinguishes you from the rest.

Famous brands tell Stories all the time!

Through Stories, the Rolex brand both makes it clear their watches are expensive and creates an Association that whoever wears Rolex has plenty of money. One of their Stories conveys the idea that a man has to have a Rolex watch by the time he is 50 years old to show he has 'made it' in life. When a man buys a Rolex – which might be his second or tenth (or hundredth!) watch – he doesn't buy it so he knows what time it is. He buys the watch to show those around him that he can afford it. It is a status item – and the Story behind the piece is more likely to sell it than the fact that it shows the time.

TAKE ACTION NOW!

Write down 3 ideas to include in the Stories you will be creating about your product or service:

1. ____

____

____

2. ____

____

____

3. ____

____

____

Tactic #12

Treat Your Customers as Part of Your Sales Team

Your customers are the best source of information to improve your offering.

Convert your customers into powerful Sales tools by asking them to recommend your services to people they know (through word of mouth and referrals). If you believe you have a good offering, it is your duty to ensure a large number of people benefit from it.

How? It's very simple: just ask them!

Happy Customers have seen the Value in what you sell. And if they see Value for themselves, they will also see Value for their friends or colleagues. **Happy Customers don't think twice about recommending you**, because they genuinely believe their friends will also benefit from your product or service.

It sometimes pays to give customers incentives to recommend you (i.e. to make sure doing so benefits them). When a guest checks out, a hotel manager might offer a 10% discount on a future night's stay in return for the guest suggesting five people he believes would enjoy your hotel. Have a form designed and hand it in to your guest on his departure. The form should request name, email and phone number. Do not ask for too much information; keep it to the bare essentials. The simpler it is for the guest to complete the form the higher the chances he will do it. If you ask too much information of your guests, they may become suspicious or feel uncomfortable.

See it in action!

This time I was the customer... on the hunt for tickets to Tony Robbins's 'Unleash the Power Within' seminar. One ticket cost $965. If you took advantage of their special offer, you paid about $600 for a ticket. But there was also the option of their permanent two-for-one special: two tickets for $965, which meant $482.50 per ticket – the lowest price you could expect to pay. The result? Keen to attend his seminar and get the best deal, I brought a friend.

What Tony Robbins achieved was to get me, a Happy Customer (as I have attended other events of his) to bring a friend (another client for him) to his event. I promoted his event to my friends, as I wanted to pay half the price for my own ticket.

You may wonder why Robbins is happy to get two people at his event for the same profit he would get from a single ticket. The answer is simple: there are no additional costs in having more people in the room, but it is highly likely that those in the room will buy his other products. For Robbins, there is Value associated with every participant at the event.

TAKE ACTION NOW!

Write down 3 ways in which you could ask Happy Customers to recommend your product to others:

1. ____________________

____

____

2. ____________________

____

____

3. ____________________

____

____

Write down 3 incentives to encourage Happy Customers to promote your product to their friends and business partners:

1. ____________________

____

____

2. ____________________

____

____

3. ____________________

____

____

Tactic #13

Market to Your Partners' Customers

Your partner's customers trust him– and will trust you by Association.

Find another company that offers services complementary to yours and has the same target market. Create a Partnership whereby you introduce the services of the other company to your customers, and the other company introduces your services to their clients. By doing this, you **increase (double) your list of potential clients.** The other company's clients are also very likely to purchase from you, if you offer ***Complementary Services***.

I offered my ***Business Doctor*** Diagnosis for free to our accountants and lawyers. They liked it, so I asked them to inform all their clients about our service, thus widening our potential customer base. Another advantage is that we come to those ***potentials*** via a trusted channel. You trust your accountant, don't you? (If you don't, it is time to change him!)

Double your prospects list overnight by having another company promote your product or service to their customers.

Here's how it's done!

You are a professional photographer who specializes in wedding pictures. You partner with a flower shop: you will refer all your clients to the flower shop and they will refer their (wedding) clients to you.

TAKE ACTION NOW!

Write down 3 potential types of companies with which you could create a Partnership (for example, accountants to promote business consulting services):

1. ______________________________
2. ______________________________
3. ______________________________

For each category above, write down 3 specific companies you will approach in the next 30 days about creating Partnerships.

Category 1:

1. ______________________________
2. ______________________________
3. ______________________________

Category 2:

1. ______________________________
2. ______________________________
3. ______________________________

Category 3:

1. ______________________________
2. ______________________________
3. ______________________________

Tactic #14

Keep in Touch with Your Customers and Prospects

An easy and quick way to Keep in Touch with your customers and prospects is via email. You might think, *Oh, customers don't want another email!* Sure, but this email will contain interesting stuff they will enjoy reading. Make sure you design your email as an extension of your visual image and fill it with interesting content for the recipient. You can send them information about how the products you sell improve their lives or how they can benefit from such products. **Keep it general; don't push your product in every email**. One offer for every three to five emails is the norm these days. (An ***Offer Email*** has a clear 'buy this now!' message and is very different to ***Educational Marketing*** – for the latter, refer to Tactic #7 'Educate Your (Potential) Customers… ')

Not sure what to send to your database? Send customers a happy birthday email, some tips, offers or discounts. How about a simple 'Welcome to our newsletter! Here's a voucher towards your next purchase'?

And yes, in order to be able to email your customer and prospects, you need to build and maintain your database; all contact details should be easily accessible. (See Tactic #23 'Keep Close to Your Customers' for more on the importance of having a comprehensive database.)

It is important to have a Strategy behind your emails. At a minimum, you need to know why you are sending that email: what is your reason for sending it, and why is it interesting for your customer / prospect to receive it?

See how we do it…

We send our subscribers regular emails with a one-minute video focusing on a tip to growing their business. Our 'why' is simply to educate our customer, to keep close to him and provide help. Such an email is called a ***Lead Nurturing Email****. The 'why' for our email subscriber is that they get a tip to improve their business; i.e. they get free business advice.*

Email marketing is the easiest way to Keep in Touch with your customers / prospects as it shows them that you care and that you want them as your allies. And what happens when people receive good treatment? They provide you with repeat business.

Various research shows that these days most people need 16 interactions with a brand to decide upon a purchase (and the number is going up every year). When it comes to dating, it has been suggested that a woman is ready to have sex after having spent about seven hours with a man of interest to her. If he asks her too quickly, she may decline. But if he gives her enough time, his chances increase significantly. The same principle applies to business: you need to warm up your target before they will say yes to you and take their credit card out of their pocket.

Remember, it's seven times cheaper to maintain a customer than to acquire a new one!

TAKE ACTION NOW!

Write down 3 topics that would be of interest to your prospects and on which you could expand in emails to them:

1. ____

____

____

2. ____

____

____

3. ____

____

____

Tactic #15

Become the Confidant of Current and Potential Customers

Free consultations / samples bring more money in the long term.

Provide free information and offer free consultations or samples to your customers. Have one person who talks to your customers and ***prospects*** and provides only great advice and information, without having to meet Sales targets. The role of this person is to be the Confidant of your prospects and current customers. She will understand exactly the Needs of your target, and help them overcome their Challenges. Then, when your customer or prospect needs the type of product you sell, he will automatically call your representative, who will pass the lead to your sales team.

Algernon, a company in Romania that sells publicity materials, has a team of Experts that visits existing and potential clients and tells them about various products available, when to use one rather than the other, what the differences are between products, how to use each product, and so on. When these ***potentials*** have any questions about promotional materials, they call their particular Expert. She is their consultant, their problem solver, their Confidante. Guess whose promotional materials she mainly recommends?

Algernon is a medium-sized company that sells across the country. Your business may not need a team of Experts – perhaps one person can do the job. Depending on the type of business you are in, this may not even be a full-time job. In that case, you may prefer to allocate one hour per day to this role, or even one hour per week. You can Delegate this task to an existing employee as a partial responsibility.

Apply this tactic to your business!

By giving samples, a perfume boutique can create a personalized Relationship with customers; i.e. become the customer's Confidant. You learn what they like and you inform them when you receive something that suits their taste. The best tactic is to call them up, have a bit of a chat and then tell them about the new arrival. They will appreciate your call (as they know you only call when you think they will like the product) and they are highly likely to buy it from you.

If you own a chocolate shop, you might have a 'VIP customers day', whereby you invite your regular customers to sample your chocolates. You then record their preferences and add this customer-specific information to your database. During those tasting events you talk to your customers and get to know them better. When an uncle's birthday approaches, you send a kind reminder to your client that she can count on you for that special surprise for her uncle.

As a professional service provider, this tactic is even easier to apply. Whether you are a landscape architect or an alternative therapist, you can offer a free half-hour consultation in which you provide Value to your potential client, but also collect information about your client's Preferences and Challenges – which you use to adapt any further communication.

TAKE ACTION NOW!

Write down 3 ideas as to how to become a Confidant to your customer(s):

1. ______________________________

____

____

2. ______________________________

____

____

3. ______________________________

____

____

Tactic #16

Write a Book...

...to be perceived as the Expert in your field.

This is my favorite tactic! As you might already have realized, I am applying it myself! Your book needn't be long and you don't have to spend your whole life researching it. Just write about your subject. After all, you are passionate about it; this is why you entered your field.

The benefits of writing a book go beyond any Sales profits you might receive for it. The book positions you as an Expert in your field, so you increase Sales of your products or services. Admit it: before picking up this book, did you know that I knew so much about business growth? Did you even know I existed?

The book can also serve as your 'brochure'. Do you know what most people do with brochures? Bin them! But would you throw a book in the bin? If you didn't consider it that interesting, you might give it to someone it could benefit or wrap it up and offer it as a Christmas gift.

You might be thinking: *I'm not an Expert in my field and I can't write a book!* Of course you are an Expert in your field. That is why you have people pay you for whatever you sell. **And this is exactly why you write a book: to be perceived as an Expert.** If it helps, find relevant people, such as case studies or other Experts to interview. Most people will receive your request well – they will end up being quoted in a book and will gain a bit of publicity for themselves.

You may say, 'I own a restaurant; I'm not a writer!' But who is stopping you from putting together a recipe book, which you can offer to your regular guests or sell in your restaurant? These days it is so easy to publish a book. Anyone can, provided there is content in that book.

Apply this tactic to your business!

I recently told a lawyer to write a book and he asked me if I had ever read a legal book. I hadn't. He said, 'Exactly! Because they are so boring.' My response was, 'Make it fun, make it interesting, make it enjoyable!' As a divorce attorney, you might write about the rather controversial subject of prenuptial agreements: how to go about them, why they are good to have, how they can save you long and unpleasant court proceedings, why they are worth the initial investment and how they can even save you money. If you also create a Story around prenuptial agreements (see Tactic #11 'Tell Stories to Sell'), you create awareness, teach people how to talk about prenups and show them how to appoint a lawyer (you!) to help them.

TAKE ACTION NOW!

Write down the topic of your book:

____

____

____

Write down 5 possible chapters of your book and the main elements for each; i.e. the main issues / subjects covered in each chapter.

1. ____

2. ____

3. ____

4. ____

5. ____

Chapter 3
Grow Your Sales

Tactic #17

Use Inducements to Close Sales Now

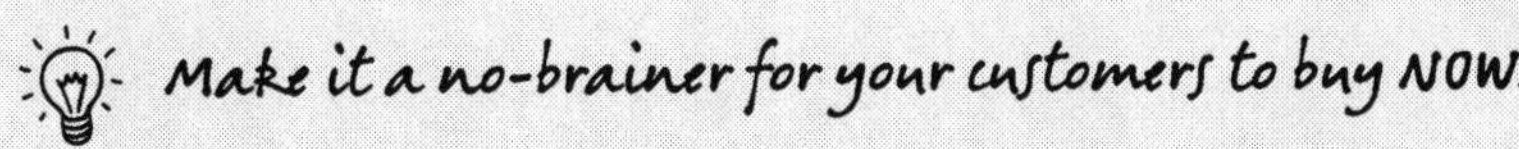

Consider offering something extra in order to close the deal on the spot. Estée Lauder introduced the idea of ***Gift with Purchase*** and Jay Abraham introduced the idea of ***Risk Reversal***, whereby the buyer can 'reverse' the transaction if she is not happy; i.e. she returns the product to the seller and gets her money back. Risk Reversal is about overcoming the client's fear or reluctance to purchase by offering to 'guarantee her purchase' and/or to refund her without any explanation being required.

By offering that something extra, you increase your closing ratio. You get those ***potentials*** who are not 100% sure about the purchase to decide on the spot. You also get those people who simply cannot take a decision to buy then and there. People may like your product, they may consider buying it, but this no guarantee of purchase. This something extra is the 'kick' they need to make the purchase.

Big brands include classic Inducements into their closing process to motivate people to buy faster or with greater enthusiasm, such as:

(i) buy one; get one free
(ii) get a second product at half price
(iii) coupons on purchase
(iv) points or rewards on purchase
(v) Gift with Purchase.

After reading this, you will notice many more examples in your daily life. You don't need to go further than your local supermarket. Use these techniques as inspiration for your own Inducements.

Risk Reversal has been used for a long time by most large stores. Usually you can get a refund for a product within 28 or 30 days. More recently, this Strategy is being used by companies that provide training courses. For example, when I signed up for the Tony Robbins Business Mastery course, I was assured – in writing, on the sign-up form – that if I did not find a million dollar's worth of Value in the course after the first day, I would receive a full refund. The four-day course cost almost as much as an MBA and this insurance helped me make my decision to buy the course. It minimized my risk. I could also get 25% of the course for free and leave after the first day with a full refund. The course was amazing, so I stayed.

Make it work for you!

You don't have to be Tony Robbins to offer insurance and use Risk Reversal. As a nutritionist, you can offer a cash back guarantee on your eating program: if your patient does not lose a certain (minimum) amount of weight within a week of applying your advice, she gets a full refund. If she doesn't lose that weight, you know she is not following your advice and don't want her as your client anyway.

TAKE ACTION NOW!

Write down 3 ideas for Inducements to close your Sales:

1. ____

____

____

2. ____

____

____

3. ____

____

____

Tactic #18

Sell More On the Spot

A customer who purchases one item from you is in 'Buying Mode'. Use this window of opportunity to sell more.

Offer your customers other products when they make a purchase, and preferably immediately after they have decided on the purchase. **Make sure you offer relevant products, whether complementary or similar.** When you look for a book on Amazon, you are shown other books purchased by customers who bought that book. Amazon uses this technique because they expect you to buy the book you are looking at, as well as one of the other books shown. Of course the books they show you are relevant to your search!

Increase sales by 80% on the spot, at point of sale.

More Sales per customer of course means overall increased Sales. You have the customer at the ready – making a purchase – so why not encourage him to make another purchase? If you offer an additional product when the customer makes the purchase, he is more likely to buy, because he is in Buying Mode. He feels like buying, so if there is something interesting for him, he will most likely buy that additional item too. Research shows that 80% of people buy additional products on the spot. This is the cheapest way to increase your Sales. Indeed, it doesn't cost you *anything* to offer another product, the client is happy, and you increase bottom line Sales.

They've put it into practice!

Recently I popped into an Estée Lauder store to buy day cream. While there, I found a body milk, which I decided to purchase. When I got to the till, the assistant pointed to a stack of boxes next to her with a combo of products and asked if I would like one. 'It's only $15 for you today,' she said. 'It is a great deal, if you consider that the mascara alone costs $10.' What do you think I did? I was in Buying Mode and it was easy to say yes. If, however, an Estée Lauder rep had come up to me in the street with the same offer I wouldn't have bought it. If I had received a newsletter from the store offering me the product I might have considered it. The effect is not as powerful as catching me while in a shopping mood and making it effortless for me to buy on the spot.

If you sell online, this tactic is a must. When someone goes towards purchase on your site, ask if they would like to add product X (a Complementary or Similar Product) as well. Research shows that if you do this correctly and appropriately, 80% of customers will add the extra product.

TAKE ACTION NOW!

Write down 3 products you could offer when your customers make a purchase. These should be products that can be added to the shopping cart immediately.

1. ____

2. ____

3. ____

Tactic #19

Turn One of Your Products into 'Attractive Premium'

Become the toy in the McDonald's Happy Meal box.

Something is an ***Attractive Premium*** if people would be happy to receive it when purchasing something else; i.e. when the product is of interest to the customers of a different product. **When your product is an Attractive Premium you don't have to sell it yourself.** It is sold by the partnering business that uses your product to sell more of their product(s).

The McDonalds Happy Meal has been a big hit for more than three decades. A simple yet effective technique sustained this success: the toy included in the food box made this menu choice irresistible to kids. It might be less straightforward for your product but you can nevertheless find your own product that is the 'toy in the food box'.

Choose one product (to start with) to be used as Attractive Premium by another business. If you sell key chains, you could come to an agreement with a car dealer to offer key chains for free to all his customers. Of course, he has to pay for your key chains whenever he sells cars (this is different from buying a number of key chains from you at the outset; he only pays you when he sells the cars).

Make it work for you!

A property developer who finds it challenging to sell his newly built units offers to add furniture to the living room and the main bedroom as part of the deal. His offer becomes more appealing for people looking to purchase a house who don't have suitable furniture (the cost of the furniture is obviously factored into the real estate price by the developer). They see the house with the furniture and this means less hassle for them. This Strategy puts this developer ahead of his Competitors, while the furniture shop gets the orders without having to do anything. Of course the furniture seller will offer his products at a discounted price to the developer, but he has zero Marketing and Sales costs for those Sales.

A car is another example of Attractive Premium that can be added to the sale of the house. Some people may be happy or able to get a loan for buying a house, but they may not be willing or able to get one for purchasing a car, in which case a house that comes with a car will be an obvious choice.

TAKE ACTION NOW!

Write down 3 of your own products that could be used as Attractive Premiums, and why. Mention whom will incorporate your products into their offering:

1. ____

2. ____

3. ____

Tactic #20

Encourage On-the-Spot Purchase via Urgency

Sell as if today is Black Friday. As if tomorrow is also Back Friday. And the day after...

Generate a sense of Urgency to encourage your ***prospects*** to purchase on the spot. Create scarcity around your product or offering: develop a Limited Edition, or a ***Limited Stock***, or just a Limited Offer (a discount that is available for a short period only, even on a long-standing product of yours) and you will see increased Sales. Black Friday is one of the greatest inventions to facilitate On-the-Spot Purchases. Shops create a sense of Urgency by offering discounts on that day only. So you, the customer, either buy then and there at a discount, or you buy in the future and pay full price.

Of course, if today is Black Friday for one product, then the next Black Friday cannot be for the same product. Black Friday is never continuous, as it will then undermine the very effect it tries to create: Urgency.

People consider buying something to satisfy a Need, but decide to buy for very different reasons. One reason customers will buy on the spot is to ensure they get the product before stock runs out. And if stock is not likely to run out, then the offer (discount) should be limited (in time or on the number of products). Doing this influences people to make a purchase they might otherwise have postponed (perhaps forever). **Urgency is one of the most important characteristics of a successful business. It helps you sell significantly more than you would otherwise.**

Why do you buy more when you go on holiday? Because you are not likely to ever go back to that shop, so the choice is between getting it now… or never. Create the same Urgency for your products and you increase Sales.

In 2013, I attended the National Achievers Congress in Amsterdam with a group of friends. The idea of this event is to provide great content for attendees, but also for the speakers to sell their products – usually further training and development programs – on the spot to a large audience. Often the speakers / sellers create a sense of Urgency by offering something for free to the first batch of customers or creating a rush to be 'accepted' into the program due to limited spaces. One of my friends noticed Robert Kiyosaki's 'Cash Flow' board game and wanted to buy it immediately. I suggested he wait to see if

Kiyosaki offered a discount the following day, when he was due to appear on stage. My friend was adamant: 'No, I want to buy it now to be sure I get it. Have you seen how people rush to buy a product when a speaker is on stage? There are only a few games available and I don't want to miss my chance.'

Of course, the sellers display a small number precisely to create Urgency for purchase. They want the audience to buy now to avoid disappointment if stock runs out. However, stock is unlikely to run out. These are 'professional sellers' and they estimate the demand at such events and stock appropriately. They want to sell the maximum volume possible and this is just one of various techniques to encourage purchase on the spot.

> ***Now we're talking!***
> *Traditionally Nokia had always sold black phones – until they launched a* ***Limited Edition*** *of the same phone, but in pink. It was the first pink phone ever and was sold out within days due to its novelty and the scarcity they had created around it. I know because I got one! I paid a premium for it but I didn't mind because I had managed to get my hands on something that others hadn't!*

Think how many coupons, vouchers or discounts you receive that are valid for 24 hours, or a week, or 'while stocks last'! See what they're doing?

TAKE ACTION NOW!

Write down 3 ideas for creating Urgency around your products / offerings:

1. ______________________________

2. ______________________________

3. ______________________________

Tactic #21

Encourage On-the-Spot Purchase via Better Offer

Add to your offering such that your offering becomes the obvious best choice even for undecided prospects.

Another reason customers buy on the spot is to *get more for the same price.* This presents another opportunity for you to increase your On-the-Spot Sales: offer a larger quantity for the same price, or a package that can be purchased for a better price than buying the products individually. This is another type of ***Limited Offer*** that induces a quick purchase decision.

They walk the talk!

Recently I made an enquiry about Infusionsoft, software that helps manage contacts and communication, design landing pages, and more. An Infusionsoft representative showed me how their software could help my business and I was clearly interested. I asked him to give me his best offer. His reply was $246 per month (instead of $299). When I said I would buy after the holidays (my original intention), he asked me to wait and put me on hold. Within a minute he came back to me with a proposal of $216 per month, including some additional benefits. The offer was valid only on that day. So I made the purchase. They had made me an offer that I could not refuse, both by decreasing the price and adding more to the product, to create a sale on the spot.

Think about your household shopping: you go to the supermarket to buy fresh bread and vegetables, and you end up also buying washing up liquid. It was a good deal: they offered a larger bottle of Fairy, with 50% more, for the regular price. So you bought the washing up liquid now, even though you had just purchased some the week before and did not need any at that time…

TAKE ACTION NOW!

Write down 3 ideas for Better Offers on your existing products / services:

1. ____
____
____

2. ____
____
____

3. ____
____
____

Tactic #22

Know Your Customers. What Keeps Them Awake at Night?

Learn about your prospect's Challenges so you are relevant to her current Needs.

Know precisely the top five issues your clients are facing. Make it your business to know the kind of information they are interested in receiving. Ensure your salespeople know the areas in which your clients would like to see improvements in their businesses or lives. Become familiar with your clients' criteria for making a decision about buying a product like yours. Make sure the information you provide is relevant, that it addresses your clients' Interests and Challenges.

Your salespeople should also know the answers to the following:

- What do I really want to accomplish in this account or discussion?
- Why are some prospects not buying from me?

Only by knowing what your prospects need are you able to satisfy them. If you don't know what they really want, how can your offer be relevant to them? The more relevant you are, the more attracted your prospects become to your business.

My clients are business owners who want to attain more customers, more money, and more time for themselves – which is why I have structured this book as I have. Each chapter addresses a Challenge that a business owner may have. My Objective with this book is to help business owners reach their Goals. I do so by providing information relevant to their Challenges. This book is a bonus – by offering it for free to my clients and selected prospects, I give them more than what they ask for. By providing them with what they need, I also create a Relationship with my prospects and clients, which also makes them more likely to buy from me. The information I provide here is relevant to my clients. If it triggers more questions and they want to know more about how to apply these techniques to their businesses, they will buy more services from my business.

By being relevant to your customers, they listen to you and are interested in what you say – via emails, newsletters and billboards, and on your website.

Why do you think online bounce rates are so high? Because visitors don't find the message relevant to them and they don't want to waste their time.

Here's why you need to do this!
A man enters a women's department store. The shop assistant asks, 'Are you looking for something special?'. She starts a discussion in order to understand what the man wants so that she can show him relevant articles. Imagine if she had suggested lovely lingerie for his girlfriend, only to discover he was celebrating his mom's 80th birthday.

TAKE ACTION NOW!

Write down 3 Challenges that your customers are facing right now:

1. ______________________________

____

____

2. ______________________________

____

____

3. ______________________________

____

____

Tactic #23

Keep Close to Your Customers

Become your customer's friend and she will become your fan.

Build your database with information about your customers and use it to Maintain Contact with them on a regular basis. If you are a retailer, collect basic information such as name and contact details. If you know their address, can you deduct their status, their spending power or the type of products they buy? (If you can't just yet, collect the addresses nonetheless and you will figure it out later.) Don't forget to collect email addresses to feed into your email marketing campaigns. Date of birth is important too – you might want to send a happy birthday voucher to show you care for them and to get them into your shop, spa, or business. Collect information about the products they buy, how often, and how much they spend in your shop. Use all this data to get closer to your customers. Inform them of products, special offers and promotions they may be interested in.

If you are a ***B2B*** company, your job is more difficult as you have to know all of the above for each contact person. You need to keep track of the people you deal with when they change jobs. Make sure you get introduced to the successor and that you know where your contact person has moved.

The more one-to-one discussions involved in the Sales process, the more crucial this information becomes. Think of your company's top 20% clients. Each company has a contact person. For each contact person, your salespeople should know: what will make them more successful as individuals, their ultimate Goal(s) in life, their hobbies, the number of children they have (and their ages and names). Basically, the sales representative has to become friends with his clients. Get to the point where you pay each other visits at home and outside of work.

The more you know about your clients, the easier it is to sell to them.

The closer you get to your customers, the more often they come to you for purchase. People do business with people they like. People are more likely to buy from a friend than from a stranger. Become friends with your customers and potentials and you have a better chance of selling to them.

The more you know about your customers, the more you can adjust your offerings, your Sales process and your approach to be relevant to them. Being relevant adds Value to their lives and increases their interest in your business. They come to you for purchase when they need the product you sell.

Nobody wants to be sold to, but everybody wants to choose to buy. So make them buy from you.

I naturally become friends with the clients I like. As a result, whenever they have a business problem they come to me for a Solution, which means another consulting contract for my company. Alternatively, if I have a Solution that I know is a good fit for certain clients, I tell them about it and there is always a good chance they will buy it.

Put it into practice!

In essence, we are all retail clients. Have you ever received an email from a retailer and bought something you weren't really looking for… because it was there, just a few clicks away. (Or perhaps you were looking for the product but hadn't started your search for it yet.) The company that sold you the product was closer to you than their Competitors, and they made the sale. Maybe you wouldn't have purchased the product at all, or maybe you would have bought from another retailer… You bought it based on proximity.

TAKE ACTION NOW!

Write down 3 ideas on how to get closer to your customers:

1. ______________________________

____

____

2. ______________________________

____

____

3. ______________________________

____

____

Tactic #24

Contact All Customers Soon after Their Purchase

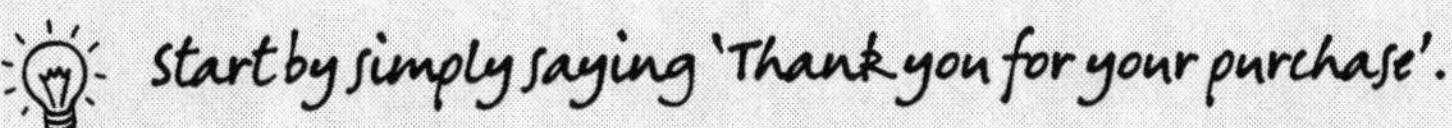

You want to Stay in Touch with customers to show you care, though the aim is also to make another sale or to get another order in the future. Contact all customers within 10 to 20 days of their initial purchase. Do this via an email, a telephone call, or a letter – whichever you are more comfortable with. You can contact them to check their level of satisfaction, to offer another product or a discount, or to inform them of new products or of the benefits of their purchase.

Keeping in Touch with your customer post purchase can be as basic as saying 'thank you'. Courtesy has multiple benefits: it nurtures the Relationship, increases brand awareness, and (ultimately) paves the way for another sale or order. By Keeping in Contact, you also remind them you exist. When they need your product again, it's you they will think of.

Once I have signed a contract with a new client, I assign him a project manager. I know my consultants do an excellent job, but I nonetheless make a courtesy call. I do this to make him feel special and to show I care. Sometimes I receive Feedback that helps me improve my services, so I get double the benefit from these calls.

If you have so many customers that you can't possibly call them all yourself, either assign a person to call on your behalf or send an email.

Make it work for you!

For a retailer, the job of following up with customers post purchase is simple. Amazon sends regular emails with relevant products based on your previous purchases. eBay sends offers to list your items for free as well as relevant products. Photo management site Shutterfly sends potential photo books (automatically designed) based on albums customers have created or offers on personalized items, such as a mug with the customer's photo. They also send special offers depending on prior purchases or lack of purchase and they always have special deals for Mother's Day, Christmas and other holidays.

TAKE ACTION NOW!

Write down 3 messages you would like to send to your customers post purchase, as well as the preferred means of communication (email, telephone, letter, postcard, etc.):

1. ____

2. ____

3. ____

Tactic #25

Develop Partnerships

Join forces with a complementary business to get bigger bang for your marketing buck.

There are various types of Partnerships that you can develop to increase Sales. We already saw the potential of marketing to your partners' customers (see Tactic #13) and the benefits of Association. One rule applies to all Partnerships: create a *win-win Relationship*. **Both parties must benefit from the Partnership.**

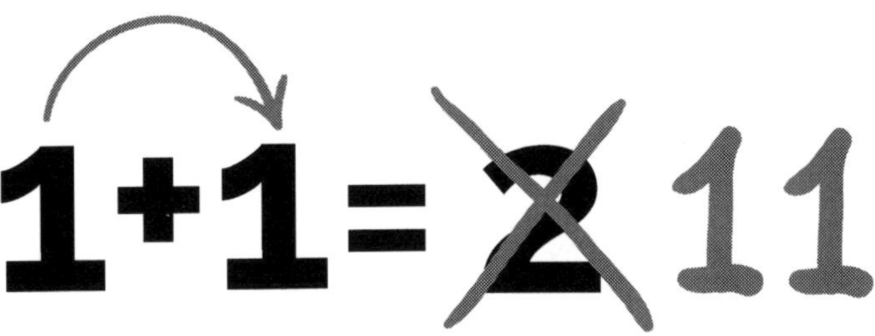

Such Partnerships help generate quicker and / or larger volumes of Sales. The effort of attracting customers is either shared between parties, or undertaken by one partner (in which case the 'passive' partner can sell more with no extra effort.) If, for example, you have a large database of customers, you can sell your partner's services to your customers and receive commission. Either way, you increase Sales, with good profit margins.

Some examples of types of Partnerships to inspire you!
Use and combine them as you like.

- ***Affiliate Marketing*** refers to a contract whereby one business reaches customers for the other business in return for a percentage of any successful Sales. Your partner has access to a large number of your customers within your target market and promotes your product for a percentage of the Sales you make from his list. This Partnership is common online, where the Affiliate partner can charge you either a percentage of the sale, or for every visitor that comes to your site from his website, newsletter or any other action he has undertaken to attract customers to you. Affiliate

marketing is a great way to quicker reach your dream clients (those clients you consider the best match for your business). For example, we sell small business growth services. So a good Affiliate Marketing partner for us would be the Small Business Association (SBA), who has a trusted relationship with many small businesses. A Partnership with SBA could give us access to their members. We would pay the SBA 10% of all Sales generated from their members. Everybody would be happy: we would get more clients and the SBA would get more income.

- ***Joint Venture (JV)*** is a business arrangement in which two or more parties agree to pool their Resources for the purpose of accomplishing a Specific Goal. This might be a new project, or simply to generate Sales for one or both parties. Our business could, for example, partner with Infusionsoft (the software company whose offer I could not refuse; see Tactic #21 'Encourage On-the-Spot Purchase via ***Better Offer***'). We both sell to small businesses and our products are complementary. By creating a JV, we could combine our efforts to attract customers for both of our businesses.
- ***Cross Selling*** involves selling one's products together with another business's Complementary Products. For example, I could create a Cross-selling Agreement whereby I offer our business growth services packaged with website diagnosis and improvement from Woorank.com. The latter is a service that we can't offer ourselves, but it is relevant to our target market, who are interested in improving their websites as part of working on attracting more customers.
- In a ***Host-parasite Relationship***, one business enters into a venture with another business with the aim of exploiting (on an ongoing basis) something valuable that the other company has – for the benefit of *both* businesses. ***Attractive Premium*** (see Tactic #19 'Turn One of Your Products into "Attractive Premium"') is an example of a Host-parasite Relationship. The premium provider relies entirely on its partner to generate the Sales.

TAKE ACTION NOW!

Write down 3 types of business with which you could create a Cross-selling Partnership. Briefly write the potential benefits to both parties:

1. ______________________________

____

____

2. ______________________________

____

____

3. ______________________________

____

____

Identify 3 types of business with which you could create a Host-parasite Relationship. Briefly write the potential benefits to both parties:

1. ______________________________

____

____

2. ______________________________

____

____

3. ______________________________

____

____

Tactic #26

Start a Relationship with Your Prospect

Offer something for free or at a low price to start a Relationship with your potential customer.

Not everyone is ready to buy right away. They may not need your product or service, or they may not trust your brand (yet). This is why you want to start building Relationships with as many potential customers as possible. Some people appreciate your information about your product or service, but others may require a taste before buying it.

Offer a free trial, or a sample of what you do. Provide Value to your prospect before you charge anything. **People like to receive free stuff, and if they have had a good experience with your brand, they are highly likely to purchase from you.**

Think of your shopping at your local supermarket... did you get to taste yoghurt, a piece of ham or a cereal? Large brands do promotions like this all the time. They want you to taste their product (for free) and usually combine this with an On-the-Spot Promotion (see Tactics #17, #20 and #21 for strategies that create On-the-Spot Purchase). The idea is that once you have tried the product – and assuming you like it – they will then give you an even better reason to immediately purchase it, either by providing more quantity for the same price or a discount. Their main aim is to get you to consume their product in the hopes that you will become a regular customer.

They're already doing it!

Most SaaS (Software as a Service) companies use this tactic successfully. They let you use their software for a month for free, or they let you use a light version of their software free of charge, with the expectation that once you know the product and like it, you will become a paying customer for its additional features. Mailchimp offers a free emailing service if you have less than 2,000 users. But when your email list grows beyond this, you have to move to a paid solution, whereby they charge you $75 (or more) a month. If you like their free service, you are likely to upgrade and pay them to send more emails to more people. Your cost of starting a Relationship with them is zero, but if you later want to move, you have a bit of work to do, so it is usually easier to stay with Mailchimp and pay for the premium product.

This tactic works well for membership sites too, where your first month, or first post, or first listing is free. I search for tenants for my flat in London via www.openrent.co.uk. The first ad is free for five days. If you are lucky enough to find a tenant in five days, you don't pay anything. After this period, your ad will remain online, but not on the main property search sites; i.e. your chances of finding a tenant are close to zero. Having experienced and enjoyed the services of www.openrent.co.uk for free, I paid to have my ad published beyond the first five days. Offering those free days had hooked me in and enabled them to start a Relationship with me. I like the service so much that I will continue to use it whenever I need tenants for my flat.

TAKE ACTION NOW!

Write down 3 potential products or services you could offer for free (i.e. as a sample) to build a Relationship with potential customers:

1. ______________________________

____

____

2. ______________________________

____

____

3. ______________________________

____

____

Tactic #27

Upgrade to a Sales Machine Organization

Offer something for free or at a low price to start a Relationship with your potential customer.

Great Sales is a matter of both personal talent and good organization. While the first is up to your sales staff and can be managed only indirectly by you, the business owner, the latter can be methodically improved by following certain simple steps.

The internal organization of your Sales function can have a make or break effect. **Improve your internal organization** by following these basic rules:

1. Have a procedure to approach and deal with ***prospects***.
2. Have weekly meetings for your sales team.

   a. Ensure your salespeople improve themselves in the weekly meetings, by sharing information, by observing what works and what doesn't work, by learning from each other, etc.

   b. Review your Sales process constantly in the weekly meetings, with the aim of improving it.
3. Analyze Customers' Feedback and constantly improve your processes.
4. Ensure you have a Reporting System that functions.
5. Allocate the most difficult Sales to your Best Performers.
6. Recruit and retain only the best.
7. Remunerate your sales team based on performance.
8. Have administrative tasks performed by admin people and allow your sales team to sell 100% of the time.
9. Personally Train the salespeople and ensure they exhibit the values you want them to have.

Your salespeople should follow the **seven steps of the selling process**:

1. Establish a rapport with the prospect. Your salespeople should spend 60% of their time on this. For example, see Tactic #22 'Know Your Customers. What Keeps Them Awake at Night?'
2. Find Need. For example, see Tactic #15 'Become the Confidant of Current and Potential Customers'.

3. Build Value around your company's offering. For example, see Tactic #11 'Tell Stories to Sell'.
4. Create desire. For example, see Tactic #26 'Start a Relationship with Your Prospect'.
5. Overcome objections. For example, see Tactic #17 'Use ***Inducements*** to Close Sales Now'.
6. Close the sale. For example, see Tactic #20 'Encourage On-the-Spot Purchase via Urgency'.
7. Follow-up. For example, see Tactic #24 'Contact All Customers Soon after Their Purchase'.

Ensure your salespeople are trusted and perceived as credible and Experts. Make sure they build ***Brand*** Loyalty, pre-empt Competitors, generate referrals and motivate action immediately. Your salespeople are the engine of your organization. Their performance reflects directly on the results of the entire company.

TAKE ACTION NOW!

Write down 5 additional characteristics you would like your Sales System to have:

1. ____

____

____

2. ____

____

____

3. ____

____

____

4. ____

____

____

5. ____

____

____

Write down the next 5 actions you will undertake to put a Sales System in place, or to improve your existing System:

1. ____

2. ____

3. ____

4. ____

5. ____

Tactic #28

Position Your Product or Service as an Exclusive Offering

Stop chasing customers. Make them chase you and your product or service.

This is my favorite Strategy. Although it is difficult to achieve, it is definitely worth the effort. In the ideal scenario your offering is so great that your target customer is clear he wants it. It is so difficult to get, though, that your potential customer wants it even more. Your potential customer has to 'qualify' to be able to buy this offering. This is where you need to get to…

The more Exclusive the product, the more desired it is – and the more willing people are to pay a premium for it. You don't have to sell Louis Vuitton bags or Jimmy Choo shoes to get there. Create this kind of brand in your own industry. Why do people pay so much for a bag or a pair of shoes? Because of the quality, the design, the style, the brand, the status associated with them… what is so special about these products apart from the aforementioned factors? *Not everyone can have them.* Exclusivity makes them even more special.

If you sell an online product, make it accessible by invite only. Get inspiration from www.asmallworld.net, a social site that offers Exclusive Deals and Events to members.

Even a *regular product* can have some extraordinary features that make it unique and can be played upon for marketing purposes. Annabel's is a club in London where you can be accepted as a member only if you get two recommendations from existing members. You can become a member only after a screening process that takes a year or more. This makes it a hugely desirable place, especially for those people who go out in London a lot and want to visit those exclusive, high society places.

Even if your product doesn't have particularly unique characteristics, brand it via Association. Look at Nespresso: it is always associated with George Clooney.

Learn from the best!

Did you know that Hermes sells certain lines of bags for tens of thousands of dollars, and that you may have to wait months to be able to buy one? Why do you think the Hermes bags are so expensive and in demand? Because there is a limited number of them. Of course, Hermes could open up a new production line to satisfy all that demand – but that is not their Strategy. You have to 'qualify' before you are able to place an order. (Anyone who wants a Hermes bag needs to first have spent a minimum of $50,000 on other purchases.) Hermes' salespeople call this 'building a relationship with Hermes', which translates as spending loads of money in a Hermes shop before you can have a bag. Hermes 'uses' their bags to sell large volumes of other (super-expensive) products they have in store.

As you might have already guessed, I am a huge fan of Tony Robbins! He too uses the tactic of creating exclusivity to sell at a premium. He offers a number of excellent products to business owners, but one needs to 'apply' or 'qualify' to be able to buy these (expensive) products; i.e. Robbins 'selects' you to spend money on his products. You are then more likely to purchase because you feel special and have 'qualified' for the Exclusive Products. And of course, now that you are finally permitted to purchase, you don't want to miss out. You might pay a premium for the product but you are happy to do so.

There is one essential condition to the success of this technique: you, like Robbins, have to be able to deliver both quality and great Value for money.

TAKE ACTION NOW!

Write down 3 ideas you could apply in your business to position yourself as Exclusive:

1. ____

____

____

2. ____

____

____

3. ____

____

____

Tactic #29

Follow Your Customer's Needs

Stay in the game. Constantly adapt your offering to the shifting Needs of your customers.

The world changes faster than we realize, and so do the Needs of your customer. Make sure you know the Needs of your customer today (see Tactic #22 'Know Your Customers. What Keeps Them Awake at Night?'), but also anticipate your customer's Needs in the near future and in the long term. Study the market and the trends, the habits, the changes in your industry and constantly adapt your product and your offering. Ensure your offering fits the current market and be ready to adapt it to meet future demands.

The advantage of adapting your offering to match demand is obvious. Less obvious is the consequences of not adapting it to the future. We have all seen new companies grow to be large and successful, and we have all seen large and successful companies go bust. **New companies are changing the rules of the game and you need to ensure you are a player in the 'new game'.**

This is why you need to adapt!

The internet may be a threat to some companies, but it is an opportunity for many more. Kodak, previously a top photographic company, is almost unheard of today, while Shutterfly, which stores photos online and offers printing services, has succeeded largely due to the internet.

We have also seen the effect of the internet on traditional businesses like media, where the rise of online news has led to a decline in printed media. If you were a media company 10 years ago, you would have to change your offering to be successful today. Now look ahead another 10 years. Do you want to get there and think: 'I wish I had seen this coming 10 years ago'?

Think of companies like Google, Groupon, Booking.com, Amazon and eBay. Big names today – yet none of these existed 30 years ago. If you are not convinced, look at your own Needs today. Are they the same as they were five years ago?

TAKE ACTION NOW!

Write down 3 Needs of your customers today:

1. ____

____

____

2. ____

____

____

3. ____

____

____

Write down 3 Possible Needs of your customers tomorrow (what you think your customers will need in future):

1. ____

____

____

2. ____

____

____

3. ____

____

____

Tactic #30

Revisit Your Lists of Past Prospects and Customers

You already have a Relationship with a former customer. Exploit it to sell more.

Take a look at all the customers and potential customers you have ever spoken to, enter them into a database and revisit them. Call, email or make an appointment with the view to exploring new ways of collaboration – by which I mean making a sale (of course), but also creating possible Partnerships, where applicable. (See Tactic #25 'Develop Partnerships' for ideas on types of Partnerships.)

You already have a Relationship with these people. As you have had one or more interactions with them in the past, you are not cold calling them per se. **Assuming these customers had a positive experience with your company, they will be happy to receive your call**. You sold to them in the past, so why not sell again? If you don't do it, your Competitors will.

Make it work for you!

I used to offer assistance with fundraising to companies that wanted to take on an investment project or business owners who wanted to sell their companies. In time, my business's Focus shifted towards helping business owners grow their companies organically, by attracting more customers and being more efficient internally, so they produced more cash flow. When I wanted to grow my new business further, I emailed all previous clients and prospects with information on my new services. Twenty-four percent responded and requested more information – that was 100 or so hot leads for the new business. In addition, I received a number of lunch invites and the chance to catch up with old contacts face to face.

TAKE ACTION NOW!

Write down 5 actions you will undertake to start communicating with former customers:

1. ______________________________
____
____

2. ______________________________
____
____

3. ______________________________
____
____

4. ______________________________
____
____

5. ______________________________
____
____

Tactic #31

Sell for Next Year, Not Just for Tomorrow

Though immediate Sales are important to the success of your business, remember to also focus your efforts on Long-term Sales. By shifting from looking only short-term to looking long-term too, you ultimately create a situation in which you don't have to worry about tomorrow's sale. Wouldn't that be great?

Nurture your ***leads*** and **potentials** so they buy at some point, if it's not going to be now. Don't disregard them just because they are not potential customers today or in the near future. Look at the customer's Long-term Value and not only at today's sale. **Develop a Long-term Perspective for best results, for the value of one Long-term Customer to your company is much greater than the initial sale**.

At times this may mean you sacrifice big Profits today for Long-term Business – for example by offering the first product for free or at a low price. (See Tactic #15 'Become the Confidant of Current and Potential Customers' and Tactic #26 'Start a Relationship with Your Prospect' for more information.) **Incentivize your customers to stay with you for the long haul**.

If you have a successful subscription-based product, I assume you offer great Value. Continue to do so and adjust to Future Needs (see Tactic #29 'Follow Your Customer's Needs') and your customers will stay with you long term. If you are not sure about the Value you offer to your customer, and people mainly buy your product on price, consider doing what many phone and internet companies do: offer a lower rate to your 'valued customers' to guarantee future Sales. Do you know what those phone and internet providers are really doing? They are giving you a discount (i.e. sacrificing profits now) in return for a two-year contract. We call this ***locking Sales*** in for the future.

Provide credit towards your customer's next purchase.

If you offer one-off products and subscriptions or contracts are not an option, you still need to give incentives for repeat business. An easy way to do this is to provide credit towards the customer's next purchase.

When I recently bought baby clothes from Osh Kosh B'gosh, the automated receipt included a 10% discount voucher – valid for a month, starting the next day – towards my next purchase. What the store did was to give me an incentive to come back within a month of my purchase. You might argue that once you've bought baby clothes, you will not need to come back. You are absolutely right. But you may suddenly consider buying a present for your friend's baby, or even giving her the 10% discount voucher.

Learn from the best!

My all-time favorite Tony Robbins masters all these techniques and more! When I bought his 18-month coaching program, it was automatically packaged with a $475 credit towards any Tony Robbins event I chose to attend in future. Robbins knows that I will have to pay more than that to attend another event, and he also knows that, by going to that event, I am more likely to buy further products from him. His offer of a credit is a way to nurture me and encourage me to stay with his company into the future.

You don't have to run a multinational to use these strategies for locking in your Sales in advance. Understand the principles and tailor them to your own business.

TAKE ACTION NOW!

Write down 5 ideas to generate Long-term Customers or Sales:

1. ______________________________

2. ______________________________

3. ______________________________

4. ______________________________

5. ______________________________

Chapter 4
Increase Internal Efficiency

Tactic #32

Automate Processes

When you repeat a task five times or more, you need to think about Automating it.

Initially, when you set up your company, you did the Sales, the customer delivery and took the trash out. Then you employed a few people and Trained them to do things the way you did. You are not a one-man show anymore; you own and run a business. But what happens when an employee leaves? Well, you recruit another person – who you have to Train. But what if you have no time to Train her, if you have taken on other responsibilities that keep you busy? Is it not better to **have processes and procedures in place** so that new recruits can easily learn (by themselves or with minimal assistance) how to do things?

So you have put processes in place. Now take this one step further… Is it not even better to Automate these processes; that is, to facilitate the process being carried out independently, by itself? (For more information on getting Technology to revolutionize your organizational processes, see Tactic #100 'Leverage with Technology'.)

This is how it's done!

Let's take invoicing as an example. You invoice a client every quarter. Initially you remember when to send the invoice out – it's your first contract, so how can you forget? Later, as you acquire more contracts, you might have someone in your company capture all contracts into an Excel spreadsheet to check and update regularly for you. But instead you could be using software that programs these invoices to be issued automatically. Better still, this software will ensure invoices are also sent to the client automatically and registered in your accounts.

Save time and costs by using Technology.

TAKE ACTION NOW!

Write down 5 actions that you (or your staff) perform five times or more:

1. ______________________________

2. ______________________________

3. ______________________________

4. ______________________________

5. ______________________________

For each action, think of at least 2 ways you could Automate it:

Action 1:

1. ______________________________
____

2. ______________________________
____

Action 2:

1. ______________________________
____

2. ______________________________
____

Action 3:

1. ______________________________
____

2. ______________________________
____

Action 4:

1. ______________________________
____

2. ______________________________
____

Action 5:

1. ______________________________
____

2. ______________________________
____

Tactic #33

Plan the Day

This is equally valid for both you and your staff. Everyone in your company should plan each day. But what about all those things that have to be done on the spot and cannot be anticipated? No problem: when you break down your day into tasks, you plan for miscellaneous activities too. **You are in control of your work and your time, and you need to schedule in those things you want to accomplish**. Otherwise you will end up answering the phone, discussing something with an employee by the coffee machine, or fighting fires. If you don't know when you will be working on specific tasks, other things will always come along that 'need to be solved urgently'. And you will never have the time to work on the tasks that are most important to you.

Include unplanned time in your planning!

If about one third of your personal assistant's day cannot be planned in advance, then she will plan the other two thirds and leave the remaining time open for on-the-spot tasks.

Put it into practice!

Good planning also involves allocating big things that take a long time into small chunks of time. (See Tactic #36 'Be Efficient with Your Time' for more on Chunking Up and Down.) In other words, break tasks that take a long time into smaller pieces that can be dealt with regularly. For example, I allocated one day per week to write this book, because I wanted to have it ready in four months.

Divide big projects into small, manageable chunks to be dealt with over time.

If your employees don't plan their day, you will never be completely satisfied with their performance. When you ask someone to do something for you, two possibilities emerge:

1. They drop everything else to do your task, in which case something else that was important will not be accomplished.
2. They carry on with their work until it is finished (if ever), before moving on to your request.

Which outcome do you prefer? I would say neither! With careful planning, your staff can follow through on their responsibilities and on your task in due time.

TAKE ACTION NOW!

Write down the most 5 important things you have to deal with. 'Important' refers to those tasks that make a difference in your business and not what is urgent. Start with the most important action down to the least important. For each action, estimate how much time you need to complete it.

1. ______________________________

____

Time required: ______________________________

2. ______________________________

____

Time required: ______________________________

3. ______________________________

____

Time required: ______________________________

4. ______________________________

____

Time required: ______________________________

5. ______________________________

____

Time required: ______________________________

If any of the tasks / actions above take more than 10 hours for you or your staff to complete, break them down into manageable steps below.

Step 1. ______________________________

____

Step 2. ______________________________

____

Step 3. ____

____

Step 4. ____

____

Step 5. ____

____

Insert the above tasks / actions – including each step to completion – into your diary and stick to them. Treat these tasks as important meetings that you cannot miss – even when the task involves working by yourself.

Tactic #34

Use Meetings

I say *use* meetings and not have meetings because the Goal is to Train everyone in your company to save issues to be discussed with the boss for scheduled meetings. The only exception to this rule is any issues that truly are urgent. **Issues that are not urgent should be put on a list and dealt with in one go during a meeting.** This tactic helps both you, the leader, and your managers have a more productive day.

If you have employees or colleagues coming into your office all the time – to ask you to sign a document, to authorize a payment, or to seek your opinion – you are constantly interrupted. To avoid this, schedule set times for these discussions. For example, your accounts person may come to you to authorize payments every day at 10 am and *not* three times a day (or whenever she feels like it). Or your product manager may come to you to discuss progress every day at 11 am and *not* every half hour (or every time he has a question or problem).

As for those urgent issues that can't be predicted, allocate an hour per day in which you take 'got a minute' meetings. So if anyone in the company has a challenge during the day, they know that your door is open between 3 and 4 pm to talk about such issues.

Find Strategic Solutions to problems.

It is also a waste of time if the same kinds of problems or issues are being discussed at these meetings. Find a Solution that puts an end to the issue; solve it for good. For example, if it is the third time that you find an employee stealing from your company, it is not enough to fire that employee. You need to put in place a System to prevent this happening again. Your reaction and solution should also be made clear in a public announcement to your company, so no one will even *think* of stealing from your company in future.

Apply these good practices to manage your time more efficiently, but also Train your managers to do the same – and you will *all* be more productive.

TAKE ACTION NOW!

List 10 actions you were asked to do by your staff in the past couple of days. Be sure to include requests that interrupted your work on other, important tasks. Once you have identified these issues, you can deal with them collectively during meetings rather than on an ad-hoc basis.

1. ______________________________

2. ______________________________

3. ______________________________

4. ______________________________

5. ______________________________

6. ______________________________

7. ______________________________

8. ______________________________

9. ______________________________

10. ______________________________

Tactic #35

Use an Agenda at Meetings

You probably have a lot of meetings – but do you achieve what you want to in those meetings? In fact, do you even know what you want to achieve from each meeting?

Make a habit of setting up your Objectives and an Agenda for each meeting.

Encourage your colleagues to set their Objectives too. You don't have to be there to have them follow good practices. Everyone in your organization should approach meetings with maximum efficiency. Otherwise, they are better off going for a drink, or taking a walk in the park!

An Agenda is good when you know the Objective of the meeting, the subjects you want to talk about, and how much time is allocated to each subject matter. Appoint someone to keep track of this and make sure you cover everything on the Agenda during the available time frame.

Go one step further and follow these simple yet powerful techniques in your meetings:

- **Take minutes.** Appoint one person who is responsible for recording the events of the meeting and for circulating this to all participants and other stakeholders (if applicable). The minutes should include the main subjects discussed and, most importantly, actions agreed upon: who does what by when. If, like me, you have a bad memory, you need something in writing to refer to after the meeting. This must be detailed enough to jog your memory. Also, anyone who missed the meeting, but is interested in the subject, should be able to understand what was discussed from the minutes.
- **Assign tasks.** There is no point writing in the minutes what was discussed if tasks are not assigned. All participants should have clarity on what they and others are responsible for after the meeting. Our minutes looks like this: 'New campaign to our prospects interested in EU funding. VL to draft a message that informs them about the status of the new funding programs. AV to send the message…' and so on.
- **Assign deadlines.** Each task has to have a time frame. Let's say you assign someone to prepare a presentation for the next client meeting. Ensurc you

have clarity on when the meeting is, and by when the person responsible is expected to finalize the presentation. Have interim deadlines if Feedback needs to be given by other members of the team. Our minutes would look something like this: 'IV to draft presentation by 22 March, OG to provide Feedback by 25 March, IV to finalize by 28 March.'

- **Assign follow-up actions.** Often you discuss various issues during your meeting and generate great ideas that you may want to implement. And then what happens? Nothing! This is why follow-up actions have to be assigned – then you know who needs to do what by when, and those people are held responsible for completing their tasks. For example: 'DC in charge of building a video campaign. He will research options to embed videos in our website, and recommend solution by 5 Apr. Campaign to be ready by 27 Apr.'
- **Monitor progress.** You have assigned responsibilities – with deadlines – but you now need to ensure people take action on their responsibilities. Appoint someone to be in charge of checking on progress, to ensure the team members are doing what they are supposed to do. Also refer to Tactic #41 'Get a Reporting System in Place'.

TAKE ACTION NOW!

Note down the next 3 meetings you have scheduled. Write the subject(s) of the meeting and with whom they are taking place.

1. ____________________

____

____

2. ____________________

____

____

3. ____________________

____

____

For each meeting, write down 5 items to be included in the Agenda.

Meeting 1:

1. ____________________

2. ____________________

3. ____________________

4. ________________________________

5. ________________________________

Meeting 2:

1. ________________________________

2. ________________________________

3. ________________________________

4. ________________________________

5. ________________________________

Meeting 3:

1. ________________________________

2. ________________________________

3. ________________________________

4. ________________________________

5. ________________________________

Tactic #36

Be Efficient with Your Time

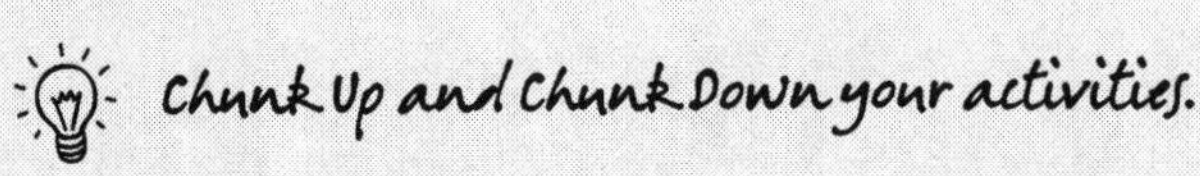

Most business people are busy. They are busy because they either like to be busy as it makes them feel important, or because they don't know any other way. The model below shows you how to accomplish much more within the same time frame. **Time is the most precious Resource you have, and it should be used wisely.**

Secret to Effective Time Management

KNOWN

Familiar activities - become second nature and a single task

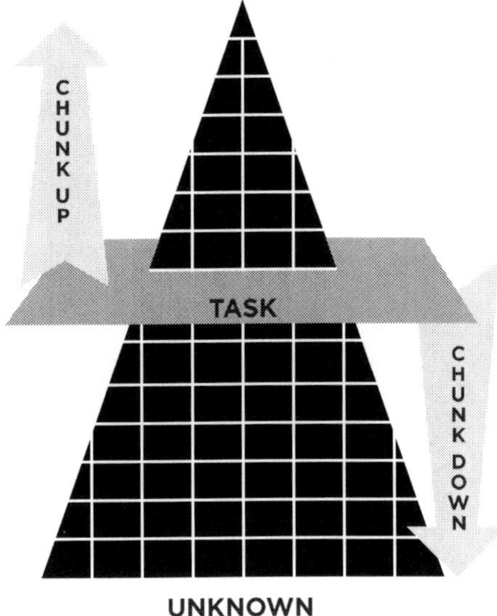

UNKNOWN

Unfamiliar activities - break down into manageable pieces

Chunking refers to breaking an activity into pieces ('chunks'). You *Chunk Up* or you *Chunk Down* depending on how known or unknown the task is to you and how comfortable you feel with that task. By Chunking Up things you know, you free up brain space. You also Delegate as a 'chunk' and have fewer responsibilities.

Chunking Down: you've seen it in action before!

When you learnt how to drive, your instructor told you to open the car door, to insert the key into the contact, to look in the rear-view mirror, to signal, press the clutch, then the accelerator and go. 'Driving' was broken down into small pieces that you could handle. Imagine how you would have reacted had someone given you the car key and said, 'Drive!' You would have felt overwhelmed and refused. Your instructor, by Chunking driving Down, made it possible – and eventually easy – for you to drive. Now that you know how to drive, driving is, well, just driving.

By Chunking Down the unknown, you make it easy for yourself to deal with that one task. You break it down into manageable pieces, which you can deal with, rather than postponing because you don't know how to start and how to handle it.

But how does Chunking Up apply in the workplace? Let's look at recruitment:

1. When you recruited your first employee, you had to publish the advertisement (after drafting the Job Description), receive CVs, read the CVs, select the ones you found appropriate, call candidates for an interview, meet them and understand whether or not they were the right fit, make notes, think about them, make a decision, make an offer to the chosen candidate, discuss again, and eventually have her sign your employment contract.
2. As you become more experienced with recruiting, you can begin to Delegate parts of this process. Once you have drafted the Job Description, your personal assistant might do the initial stages so that you become involved again later when you meet the candidates. Then your PA drafts the offer and deals with the new recruit. By doing this you have moved the task from being totally Chunked Down towards the middle of the scale, where your role is limited to Job Description, interview, and final decision; i.e. only three 'chunks' for you. The rest is Delegated to your assistant.
3. When you have someone else in the company that can handle the entire process (let's call her Anca), your task becomes: 'Anca, please recruit one more Business Doctor Consultant'. You have just one task. You have Chunked it all the way Up!

By Chunking Up things you know, you free up brain space, as they become one activity that eventually gets Delegated to others.

TAKE ACTION NOW!

Write down 3 activities with which you are familiar and which you could Chunk Up:

1. ____

____

____

2. ____

____

____

3. ____

____

____

Write down 3 activities you find difficult to deal with. Each of these activities can then be Chunked Down.

1. ____

____

____

2. ____

____

____

3. ____

____

____

Now identify a person within your company to whom you can Delegate each of the above activities.

Tactic #37

Strengthen the Weakest Link

Fix the crack, not the leak! Your business is only as strong as its Weakest Link.

The strength of any System depends on its weakest component. In a business, that may be an employee, a procedure, a process, a System, an activity… **The Weakest Link is the area or individual with the lowest level of performance.**

A few years ago, I was heading home from the seaside in my BMW. Just 20 kilometers into the journey, I noticed a red light on the dashboard, indicating the car was over-heating (my 'leak'). I realized the radiator seal had broken (the 'crack'), which means the engine would no longer cool off and driving was too risky. The fact that the car was brand new, had good acceleration, good suspension (and good everything else) did not matter. The car could not do the job it was meant to do. I could not get home. I could not reach my destination. In the end, a tow truck took my car and me back to Bucharest; i.e. I moved to 'another company' to satisfy my need to get home. Of course, had I taken the car for a service before my trip, I would have known the radiator seal was broken. I would have replaced it and reached my destination in the manner planned.

Imagine your business is a car. If one part of the organization (one link) doesn't work as it should, and your whole organization does not reach its destination as a result, you have failed to meet your Objectives. Your Weakest Link is holding you back from achieving what you want.

The key is to identify the real Weakest Link – and fix it.

In the context of an organization, the Weakest Link could be one employee who does not deliver and causes delays in delivering your product to the customer. Or the Weakest Link could be a procedure that doesn't work, or a function that is not structured well enough to deliver Value.

Apply this tactic to your business!

You have a really great product, yet your Sales are low because you simply don't know how to sell. Your Sales function is your Weakest Link. Or the contrary: you sell a lot, but your clients are not happy, because you are not able to deliver appropriately. This is because you don't have the System or the people in place to deliver according to your promises.

Whatever it is, you need to fix the Weakest Link. Then you identify the next Weakest Link, and so on. Although there is always room for improvement, don't work on improving what you are already doing well. If you sell a lot but can't deliver, it doesn't make any sense to hire more salespeople. You need to address the delivery function, as it is bringing down your performance. This is precisely why, in our Tooliers® Diagnostic Reports, we invite clients to work on the dimension with the lowest score – this is the Weakest Link of the area analyzed.

TAKE ACTION NOW!

Write down the 5 Weakest Links in your business and at least one possible Solution for each:

1. ____

____

____

2. ____

____

____

3. ____

____

____

4. ____

____

____

5. ____

____

____

Tactic #38

Eliminate Wasting Time in Routine Tasks

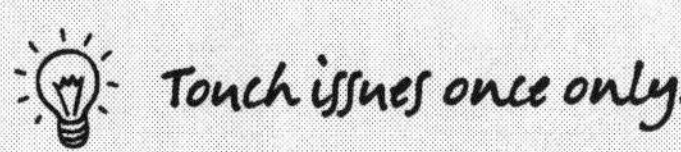

Touching an Issue refers to each time you 'visit' the issue before solving it. When an email is received, it may be opened to read, opened again to save the document attached, again to forward it, then to answer it and perhaps once more to file it. This is 'Touching' that issue *five times.* **Ideally an issue should be touched only once before it is solved.**

Here's how not to do it!

After being involved in a car accident in Romania, the other party and I went to the police station to report the incident. The police officer accompanied us outside to look at the two damaged cars, before we went back inside to sort out the paperwork. First he asked for our driver's licenses and car papers. He took one driver's license, looked at it, put in on his desk. He took the other license, looked at it, put it on his desk. Then he went to fetch the relevant documents. Next he took my declaration, then the other driver's declaration. Then he looked again at my license, and again at the other license.

He then went to get a paper clip to hold together his three documents. On his return, he looked at each driving license again. Then he took my declaration again. Then he took the other driver's declaration again. Eventually he took my license again to copy information to his document and did the same for the other driver. After more of the same, we went outside again, this time for him to take photos of the cars. Back inside, he looked again at our licenses and... you get my point.

It took him over an hour to fill in the forms; it could have been done in five minutes. Go back and count how many times he touched our papers. If he had touched each paper once, the entire process would have been over quickly.

Why waste an hour on something you can do in five minutes? If the police officer in the example above had taken five minutes, he could have dealt with 11 more cases by the end of that hour. Instead he preferred to make others wait a few hours before he started dealing with them. Maybe that made him feel important, but, as a business owner, you want to be efficient. Your importance comes from you being able to achieve the results you want, not from being busy. And the same goes for your team.

Have all your documents stored in your computer such that any document is within a maximum of five clicks away. Why would you want to waste time on opening loads of folders over and over again?

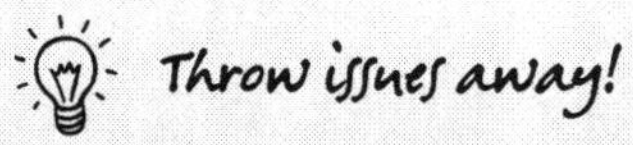

Throwing Issues Away means getting rid of issues that are of no importance; issues that are irrelevant or make no difference to the results you are after.

These tactics are valid for your entire company – not just for you alone.

Here's how it's done!

You drafted an internal document to be used for one meeting and never to be referred to again. Do you want to spend half a day putting your nice logo and branding on that document, or would like to you skip this, and just get the information down, circulate it and move on? You 'Throw Away' the unnecessary work on this document, as it does not make any difference to your results.

TAKE ACTION NOW!

Write down the 5 Weakest Links in your business and at least one possible Solution for each:

1. ____

____

____

2. ____

____

____

3. ____

____

____

4. ____

____

____

5. ____

____

____

Tactic #39

Get Used to Delegating – Properly

You already know that by Delegating you save time, achieve more, and grow your professional and business Value. You can multiple your results many times over once you start Delegating. You also know you can't do everything by yourself, for two reasons: you don't have the time to do everything and you don't always have the relevant skills or abilities.

Your time is your most precious commodity. Think how much you could do if you quadrupled your time. Well, you have the Resources: your employees. It is time to start Delegating.

Make sure each job is being done by the person most qualified to do it. If necessary, bring someone in.

Divide and conquer! Identify the tasks that others within your company can do as well as you. These are often routine tasks that do not require high-level skills or tasks that can be accomplished by someone else in your team.

Apply this to your business too!

As a consultant, I was often preparing business plans for our clients. Today I have Trained different people to (i) write those plans and (ii) develop the financial model and forecast the financial results. For a while I had to review their tasks. Today they have made such progress that I do not bring any more value by revising their work.

As a business owner, I used to buy the office supplies myself, so that I could be sure of buying what I liked. I have since learnt to allow the driver to do the shopping. Who cares if the toilet paper is blue or yellow? I have learnt to not be so particular about things that do not bring much value, so that I can concentrate on those things that do matter for the business's growth.

By Delegating routine work you will have both less stress and more time to do work that matters the most. Having extra time will enable you to take on more challenging tasks and grow both as a leader and as a professional.

If you don't Delegate, you have to accept that your hourly rate will essentially be

that of the person who can do the job. If you buy your own office supplies, you are then worth $10 per hour – or whatever you could pay someone else to do that job.

Make it work for you!

If you were a construction company owner, would you rather:

- *come up with the engineering plan for a five-story building, build the foundation, carry the bricks and take the trash out for the next three years, or*
- *hire an engineer to come up with the plan, build a team, assign responsibilities, hold people Accountable for results and have the whole building finished within three months? Engineer – to come up with the plan, bricklayers – to build the foundation, workers – to take the trash out… You know your skillset is beyond taking the trash out, right?*

How many $10-an-hour jobs are you currently doing?

TAKE ACTION NOW!

List 10 actions you perform that would cost $10 per hour. Once you have identified them, get rid of them. Delegate these actions to people who cost less than you do.

1. ______________________________

2. ______________________________

3. ______________________________

4. ______________________________

5. ______________________________

6. ______________________________

7. ______________________________

8. ______________________________

9. ______________________________

10. ______________________________

Tactic #40

Hold People Accountable to Their Responsibilities

It is your responsibility as the business owner to make it clear what you want, and to hold people responsible for what you want them to do. Focus on results. You want the job done, so this should matter to you.

People avoid taking on responsibility for various reasons. They may be afraid of failure, feel overwhelmed by the scope of the project, or just feel lazy. As their leader, you need to Motivate them, encourage them and ensure they can deliver according to your expectations. As soon as you became a leader (manager, boss, founder) you stopped being a regular employee. You are now a coach. Coaches must understand the importance of inspiring, teaching, and taking pride in teams attaining your Business Goals.

As a consultant, the number one thing I've learned is that entrepreneurs need to learn to Delegate. Do it efficiently and consistently. (See also Tactic #39 'Get Used to Delegating – Properly'.) Break down complex projects and plans into specific attainable tasks, assign those to your team members and hold them Accountable for the results – both meeting deadlines and quality of the work.

When you Delegate, tell people exactly what you expect from them, when their task is finished, and by when they have to finish it.

It is not enough though to say: 'Do this for me.' You need to ensure your employee understands what she needs to do and knows how to go about it, by when she needs to accomplish it and its importance. Are your employees making mistakes? Teach them. Losing Motivation? Delve into it: understand why; make corrections; cheer them up! Did your employees successfully reach their Goals? Share the victory and pride. They are your team.

Here's why you need to do this!

When we started Tooliers®, our online platform with business growth tools for small businesses, I asked one of my consultants to find an e-commerce (payment) solution for the project. Although we use the internet every day to buy things, none of us knows what a payment transaction really involves. I also told him to do this within a week, or we wouldn't be able to sell online; i.e. the reason, deadline and importance of the task were clear. But, two months later we still didn't have a payment solution in place. Why? Because he had to learn about online payments, to understand how the whole system works, to identify potential providers, to choose the best. This part was still relatively easy… next we had to apply for the payment processor to accept us. We even had to pay for our application to be considered. When we were rejected, we had to go back to square one and identify the next company we wanted to work with.

My colleague knew what he had to do and what result we required. However, because it was a completely new task, he could not deliver in time. I have to take responsibility for the mistake here, because I underestimated what the task involved.

When you want people to be responsible for their tasks, ensure you understand what it takes to accomplish that task, and assign a realistic time frame.

TAKE ACTION NOW!

Write down 5 actions you will take to improve the way you Delegate to ensure best delivery and as little involvement on your part as possible.

1. ________________________________

2. ________________________________

3. ________________________________

4. ________________________________

5. ________________________________

Tactic #41

Get a Reporting System in Place

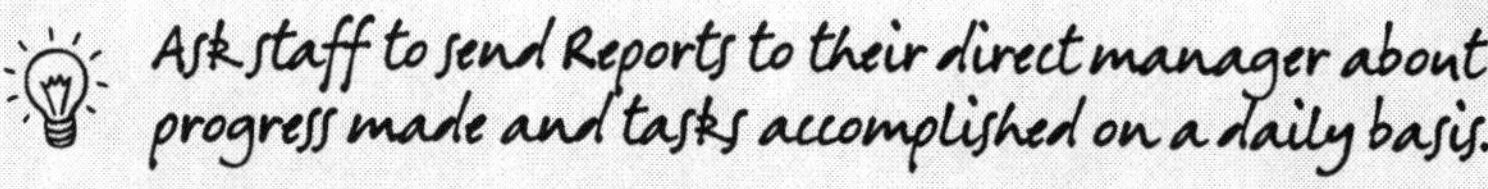

A lot of people ask me how I manage my company when I spend so much of my time traveling and very few weeks of the year in the office with my staff. The answer is simple: I assign specific responsibilities to people and I hold them Accountable. But it is the how that is the key to this working. I ask all my staff to send me a Daily Report of what they have done. This is just a simple email, so they don't have to waste a lot of time on it, and contains what they have accomplished that day, what they need to do, any problems and proposed solutions, and where they seek my response.

The Reports follow this structure:

- **Tasks done.** This section includes only tasks that are totally finished and do not require further attention.
- **In progress.** This section includes tasks that have been started but not finished.
- **To do.** These are tasks that they have not started working on.

All tasks are prioritized and deadlines are assigned to each task. By doing this, I ensure my staff deal with the most important and urgent tasks first, rather than with whatever they like most. In addition, I know every day where they are, and how they make progress, within a minute – all I have to do is open a few emails.

Do it like this!

A consultant assigned to draft a Business Plan for a client would enter under to do: 'Business Plan for Client X. AB to do financials. Deadline 10 May.' This tells me that the consultant is fully responsible for the Business Plan, but uses AB (another consultant) to do the financial section. When the consultant starts working on the project, she will move the task to In progress. Here, she might write: 'Collected 60% of the info from client; intro and market section finished.' As she progresses, she will have completed more sub-sections. The task is moved to Done only after it has been delivered to the customer; i.e. not when it is done but still in her computer.

This tactic is a way to ensure everyone in the company delivers, as they know what they have to work on, and by when. These Reports include 'to do lists', which are useful both for me and for them. Whenever they have a new responsibility, they add it to their Report. This way, I know they are responsible for that task, and that they have assumed responsibility.

TAKE ACTION NOW!

Write down 5 actions that you will undertake to get a clearer picture of i) what is happening in your company (no matter where you are) and ii) how you could contribute in the most efficient manner.

1. ____

____

____

2. ____

____

____

3. ____

____

____

4. ____

____

____

5. ____

____

____

Tactic #42

Measure Everything and Continuously Improve

Don't obsess with finding the best or most accurate Performance Indicators in the world. Simply help your team continuously improve.

You don't need complex KPIs (Key Performance Indicators) and sophisticated Performance Management Systems to review performance. If you have them, rather see KPIs as a way of being Accountable and of having your staff be Accountable – to ensure people deliver according to your Expectations. KPIs or not, you do need to have enough controls in place to measure, track and, above all, encourage performance and efficiency at all levels within your company.

You can't afford to pay people that do not deliver. Nor can you afford to do their job.

No matter how small or big your company, you need to consider some general principles when measuring performance and effectiveness. Start with your Strategic Objectives. For each major line of business, identify the most relevant indicators.

Putting it into practice!

My Objective is to achieve $1 million in online Sales in the next 12 months.

- **Q1:** *In the first quarter I am not concerned about the Sales at all. My Priority is to have the product offering perfect and the communication well set up. I could measure weekly how many email campaigns I have set up as well as how many social media followers I have. I am also interested in the number of people signing up for our newsletter and the number of people that express interest in our business by giving us their email address.*
- **Q2:** *In the next quarter, I want to see some Sales – say $10,000. The crucial indicator is now conversion on the site. How many emails do I need to send to get one sale? How much do I spend on Facebook ads compared to Google AdWords before making a sale? Each separate activity has to be measured to see which campaigns perform better. I could also look at how much time my employees spend on setting up a campaign and compare this to time required for sending messages on LinkedIn, which, although free,*

does require time. Bottom line: I want to know my Costs versus Sales for each Sales channel.

- **Q3:** *During the next quarter I am interested in improving conversions and in generating more traffic, so I look at the number of paying customers versus the total number of visitors. I also look at the best channels through which to bring visitors to the site.*
- **Q4:** *It is only now that I am concerned about Sales and want to increase the sale per marketing dollar spent.*

You probably have different people doing different jobs, in which case you need to assess them against different indicators. Use Core Indicators (five to six core competencies common to the entire team), as well as Specific Indicators to account for the specifics of each job. Involve each person or team in choosing the right yardsticks.

I bet you use revenues or Sales to check whether you are on the right track. That's good, but not enough. Numerical indicators never tell the whole story (nor do technical skills.) Good Sales are a strong indicator of an effective sales force, but they show to a lesser extent how well your product developer did her job. Assign weights to the indicators (i.e. one indicator may count twice as another, because it is more important) and consider the most relevant ones for each job or function. If your salesperson is not that good with details, don't overreact. For her it is more important to follow-up on her leads, to be a good negotiator, and to close deals. Place a heavier weight on the most relevant skills or behaviors for each person… and also understand why things don't work as planned. That is, if the product doesn't have the characteristics that the market seeks, it is not the salesperson's fault, but that of the product development staff.

In my point of view, for small businesses, Performance Management Systems (using KPIs) don't really matter that much. **You may be surprised to learn that Soft Skills and Organizational Culture can greatly impact the effectiveness and productivity of your team**. Continuous Feedback and an open Culture based on sharing the lessons learnt and guiding each other to improve can help more than the most sophisticated and expensive system in the world.

Soft Skills are hard to assess – and harder to do without. I challenge you to also consider the following when you assess the performance of your team:

- Consistently completing high-quality work on time
- Collaborating with each other to hit deadlines

- Persuading others to consider different points of view
- Appreciating the customer's perspective and his point of view
- Coaching and being coached on technical and non-technical matters
- Working successfully for a variety of managers, each with their own unique style
- Remaining flexible enough to handle rapidly changing requirements
- Making tough decisions with limited information and often dealing with ambiguity
- Challenging conventional wisdom and authority
- Helping team members who are struggling
- Taking over a project that's in trouble without being told to do so
- Managing multiple projects to a timeline
- Meeting budget restraints
- Prioritizing important tasks

Once have a good Performance Evaluation System in place, shift your Focus towards using this system to *improve your business.* Focus your mind on how your employees can help each other to improve overall performance. Observe what the Best Performers do, and try to get the Worst Performers to do the same.

Get the Worst Performers to emulate the Best Performers.

TAKE ACTION NOW!

Identify 5 areas you would like to measure in the next year. For each area, write down how you will measure it:

1. ______________________________
____
____

2. ______________________________
____
____

3. ______________________________
____
____

4. ______________________________
____
____

5. ______________________________
____
____

Tactic #43

Have an Organizational Chart

An Organizational Chart clearly shows all the positions within the company, and the people in those positions. It also shows hierarchy and reporting lines. Everybody in the company needs to know their responsibilities, how they fit into the whole picture, and whom they need to work with.

You also need a Job Description for each employee. This document records the responsibilities of the employee, and a few other important factors. We have the following items in our Job Descriptions:

- Department
- Position
- Name
- Hierarchical relationship. Here we record the people he reports to, but also his subordinates.
- Backed-up by... If he is on holiday or absent for any reason, there should be a person on hand to do his job. This is important information, because this person has to know his job, and also has to be updated on what he has done, where things are at, and so on.
- Back-up for. He could be a back-up to one person for some types of responsibilities and to another person for other types of responsibilities.
- Approved by and agreed by [the person that drafted his Job Description, and the person whose Job Description it is]
- Signatures of both persons
- Duties and responsibilities. This area details what he is responsible for.
- Knowledge and skills required. This is mainly used when we recruit someone.

I would imagine things change continuously in your company. You acquire a new employee, you create a new department, or people take on more responsibilities. Be sure to update your Organizational Chart and Job Descriptions regularly. (I do this at least once a year.) **Consider involving your team in elaborating on the Organizational Chart and Job Descriptions to increase job ownership.**

Periodically upgrade your Organizational Chart and Job Descriptions.

TAKE ACTION NOW!

Write down when you last updated your Organizational Chart:

____

Write down any changes since the last update:

1. ____
2. ____
3. ____
4. ____
5. ____
6. ____
7. ____
8. ____
9. ____
10. ____

Tactic #44

Have a Consistency System in Place

You are a company, a unit. You want your people to perform in a particular, united way.

Imagine your flight has been cancelled due to bad weather. The airport is a mess, because all other flights have been cancelled too. There are long queues to all counters. You manage to speak to someone working for your airline company and she tells you to go and make your own arrangements and that the airline company will reimburse your expenses. On your way out, you bump into another person working for the same airline company and check that you're doing the right thing. She tells you that if you make your own arrangements, you will not be reimbursed. What do you do? You get angry and feel even more frustrated. You consider going back to stand in line, but you've lost your place and would have to start at the back again.

Yes, this is a true story. It happened to me when I was flying from Vegas to Brussels, and London was a mess due to fog. Airline representatives were trying to get us out of the airport to reduce the chaos. The point, however, is that you don't want your customers to get conflicting responses from your staff. You want everyone who works for you to represent the company in an unswerving manner. **You want all your employees to perform each aspect of their job with a degree of excellence and Consistency.** You want to get predictable results, because Training and Skills are Consistent.

To create Consistency, you need to ensure that:

- Each supervisor would give a similar answer to a particular question or problem.
- Each employee would give a similar answer to a particular question or problem.
- Client treatment is similar, regardless of who is dealing with the client.
- All staff members know what is considered good performance and attitude.

TAKE ACTION NOW!

Write down 5 ideas you can implement in your company to improve Consistency:

1. ______________________________

____

____

2. ______________________________

____

____

3. ______________________________

____

____

4. ______________________________

____

____

5. ______________________________

____

____

Chapter 5
Get the Most out of Your Team

Tactic #45

Maximize Your Team's Commitment

Happy and cared for employees + committed employees = better results.

Keeping your staff committed should be one of your Priorities. When people are committed they will put in the time, effort and energy to achieve the results expected of them. When they are not committed they will do the minimum possible, waiting for the time to pass before they get their paycheck.

Employee Engagement is a key factor for your business's success and directly impacts productivity and employee retention. But what is Employee Engagement? I think of it as a meaningful two-way relationship: commitment from the employee to the company and care by the company for employee. A 2012 Gallup study suggests that only 30% of U.S. employees are engaged at work, and barely 13% of employees worldwide are engaged. Yet a happy employee delivers better results and for a longer period of time.

The tricky part though is that the recipe for happiness differs from one person to another. As the owner / leader it is your responsibility to consider each individual's particularities. Don't for a moment think that everyone is Motivated by money. If they were, they would have set up their own company (or become mercenaries!). Today's employees expect a partnership with their employer / company. They can't be treated merely as bodies or numbers (even if this is how you think of them privately).

You may retort that you allocated a budget to your managers to take their teams for lunch once a month – and this is more than any other company in your industry does. You may be right, but do you have any idea what they talk about during that lunch? Do they all bitch and moan about their job or do they talk about movies? Or does the manager take her time to understand what Motivates her team members, what they expect from the company, what their dreams are, and who they really are?

Take a step back and reflect on how Motivated the managers in your company are... how 'engaged' they are with your business. You are unlikely to have highly Motivated people in your company if their managers are not Motivated. **Ensure that all key influencers in your business walk their talk and set a good example of commitment to the rest of the staff.**

Make it work for you!

Imagine a team in which direct supervisors observe members in action, ask for Feedback, identify the root causes of employee concerns, and then follow through with meaningful improvements. Happier, more engaged employees = great results.

Now imagine a team in which supervisors talk about building Employee Engagement but in reality are simply pushing people without providing support, guiding them, or taking an interest in their personal and career development. Unhappy and disengaged employees = poor results.

TAKE ACTION NOW!

Write down 5 ways you could make your team members happier:

1. ______________________________
____
____

2. ______________________________
____
____

3. ______________________________
____
____

4. ______________________________
____
____

5. ______________________________
____
____

Tactic #46

Attract the Right Mix

Have a balanced team, with complementary skills, knowledge and personalities.

Attract the right people. I didn't say the best people! Depending on your personality, you, the entrepreneur, might want either top players (for whom you must be prepared to pay the price), or a team of low-costs employees. Neither extreme is ideal. Not all the jobs require super knowledge and super personality so hiring Superstars exclusively makes no sense. Conversely, prioritizing low cost above everything else will only attract poorly skilled and poorly qualified people.

There are three types of people:

- A players are the Superstars, the overachievers, the best candidates, the highest performers;
- B players are the average, but acceptable performers;
- C players are sub-standard performers, usually the regular guy that no one in the company notices or cares about.

Having a mix of A and B players is ideal. Have A players for the key positions within your company and choose B players for the rest. This represents the best skill / cost mix. Plus, these balanced teams are more cohesive and functional than teams in which everybody competes to become Number One. Look for the right person for each job but also make sure you have complementary skills, knowledge and personalities.

Don't waste Resources on hiring, keeping and putting up with the high demands of an army of super performers. You don't need only generals and captains in your company. Just because you like people like yourself – born leaders – doesn't mean this is a recipe for success. On the other hand, don't keep under-performers (C players) unless you see clear potential. Their salaries might be small, but don't forget about your Training costs and, more importantly, the cost of having your Superstars spending time with them instead of delivering to the top of their game for the business.

C players cost you more even if you pay them less.

Now that you understand the Right Mix in terms of performance level, consider what type of person you require for each job and be ready to make some compromises. For the management of marketing activities you want someone who understands marketing (of course) and is good at coordinating and getting the most out of her team members, be it external or internal. But for the person responsible for the marketing messages, you may need a creative person, who doesn't necessarily have to be that organized. Compromising on what is not important (organizational skills in the latter example) for each job, each hire, is a great way to get the right people.

You do not need a Superstar to clean the office, but you do want your cleaning staff to have common sense. Why? Because if they don't, you or your personnel manager will spend an enormous amount of time managing this person: showing her where to clean, what to do and how to do it. Constantly checking on the cleaning staff becomes an expensive waste of management's time. Ultimately this may cost you more than paying a better salary to someone who can get on with the job without supervision, think for herself, and anticipate what your staff need.

The next step is to get your managers to place the right work, in the right quantities, on each employee's plate. Align the responsibilities of each employee with their skills, as well as their personal interests, talents and career plans. This way your employees are happier and perform better. Doing less than that (or the complete opposite) is like swimming against the tide.

Here's why you need to do this!

When my son was born, I hired a live-in nanny to help look after him, as well as do the cleaning, cooking and general taking care of the house. She was fantastic with my son and excellent at everything else she had to do. She had empathy and she could anticipate our Needs; she would always plan ahead and make sure we had food in the fridge; the house was always tidy and clean. I didn't know what she was doing when, but I knew things were being done. As I did not have to devote any time to managing her, I could concentrate on work. When I my son was two years old, the nanny had to go back home for few months, so we hired another (temporary) nanny. She asked for 30% less than the previous one and she ate less, so our overall cost was less. However, though she was fantastic with my son, she was not as organized and prompt with the rest of her tasks. For example, she was unable to draw up an accurate shopping list for me. She would forget certain items, or put things on the list that we didn't need. The result was that I had to dedicate time to managing her and to keeping an eye on what was going on. Though our costs were lower, I looked forward to the return of our regular nanny so that I could again free up my mind and my time to do what is important: my work. This is where I add the most Value, not in checking to see if we have enough soap in the house until the next shopping trip.

TAKE ACTION NOW!

Think of your core team. Write down 5 capabilities you don't feel are at an optimal level. How can you fill each gap? Write down your ideas below:

1. ____________________

____

____

2. ____________________

____

____

3. ____________________

____

____

4. ____________________

____

____

5. ____________________

____

____

Tactic #47

Retain Those Who Fit In

Say no – even to highly skilled people – if they don't match your business's Culture.

You worked hard to build a Company Culture that represents you. You want to maintain this Culture moving forward. Thus, always take into account the personality of the individuals you recruit, and don't compromise on personal traits for skills.

Understand what is important for your company's Culture, and make that a must in new recruits. It could be positive attitude, fun, open, transparent, honest, keen to learn, open to New Ideas, likes challenges, self-starter… whatever it is, make sure that the new recruits fit the bill.

Not the right person…

A couple of years ago I got a very senior consultant, extremely skilled and knowledgeable, to join the team and manage the Business Doctor division. He may have been full of knowledge, but he was not willing to share that knowledge with my team. He soon found that none of my staff accepted him, and he had to leave. An unofficial alliance was formed against him and, believe it or not, I took their side. If that consultant was not accepted by my team, it is likely that he would not be liked by my clients or partners. And why would I want to force my team to be managed by someone they don't like? They are wonderful, it is fun to be in the office, they help each other, and I want this open and transparent Culture to be maintained. With that new person, I could see a senseless competition being played out among my colleagues, who would constantly be watching their backs – something I am totally against.

I have a policy that I only offer long-term (unlimited) employment contracts after a three-month trial period. During that initial period I want to test the skills, but also the attitude, the cultural fit, of that potential employee. If there is no match, there is no long-term contract. My team plays a role too: they vote on whether the person should stay. If they say no, it is a no. I never go against their verdict. They spend more time in the office than I do, and will be in the company of the new recruit, more than I will. And they need to be happy.

TAKE ACTION NOW!

Identify 3 people in your company that you don't feel are the right match for the Culture you want to create.

1. ______________________________

2. ______________________________

3. ______________________________

For each person, write down how you could deal with this.

Person 1:

____

____

____

Person 2:

____

____

____

Person 3:

____

____

____

Tactic #48

Ensure that Your Employees Know What the Company Expects of Them

Show the way... don't just lead the way.

Making the best strategies, business plans, job descriptions and internal procedures is a waste of your energy if you take communication for granted. These are just scrap paper if you and your managers are not equally concerned about communicating your Objectives and Expectations in an efficient and consistent manner to everyone within the company.

Business Priorities and Performance Objectives should be on everybody's lips, not lying forgotten in your manager's desk drawer.

Knowing the company's Expectations enables people to meet them; getting them involved in defining the Expectations greatly increases their Motivation. After all, your employees are also human beings with a desire to be a part of something! Okay, you don't have to ask them to set your business's Objectives, but you can (and should) at the very least share the Objectives with them and you can ask them to contribute on how to get there. You might argue: 'But the person loading and unloading the merchandise from the truck doesn't need to contribute ideas on how to create a 30% Sales increase next year!' You are right, but the sales manager should be involved, and there are probably a few other people that you don't currently involve in your planning who could help. As for the worker, he needs to know at least that you want to increase Sales by 30% in the next 12 months, and that you plan to do it by changing A, B, and C, which reflects in his job being slightly adjusted and him loading 15% more trucks.

Business owners often falsely assume that their Expectations are known once they are written in an official document or agreed upon in a formal (or informal) meeting with our managers or key people. Even worse, we tend to assume that when we have something in our heads, it has reached everyone else in the company, and they should be executing it.

Chaos or structure? Your choice!

Imagine a marathon in which there are no signs. At the start, people run straight, as is human nature, but what happens when they hit a cross road? They may stop running completely or run off in different directions. Is this how you want your staff to behave? Or would you prefer them to know what they have to do even (when you are not there)?

Now let's take the above example one step further (but assume our marathon route is obvious to the participants): when do the runners get recognition for their efforts? At the finish line? Sure, but it is the cheering along the way that Motivates them to reach the finish line!

Ask for clear results and constantly show staff how their role (however small) contributes to a Larger Business Goal.

TAKE ACTION NOW!

Write down 5 ideas you will implement in the next 30 days that will:
i) make your business Goals and Vision clearer to your staff, and
ii) enable them to see how their work contributes to achieving this Vision.

1. ____

2. ____

3. ____

4. ____

5. ____

Tactic #49

Ensure Your Employees Know Your Company's

... and encourage them to constantly seek better ways to create Value for your customers.

Do your people know what the Purpose of your business is? It's tempting to give the blunt, if a little cheesy, answer that businesses are here to make profits by means of creating Value for their customers. Ask.com describes the main purpose of a business organization as 'to serve and gratify its customers whilst making profits. Another Purpose is to achieve the Goals and Objectives as indicated within the organization's Vision Statement with its mission statement indicating how these Goals will be achieved and met'.

But let's dig a bit deeper. Try this quick reality check. How many of your employees do you think can answer the following questions?

- How does the company create Value for the customer and society?
- How does my work generally contribute to this Purpose?
- How does my work today contribute to this Purpose?
- How can I test which part of my job is directly contributing to the big Purpose and which activities are just ineffective routine (i.e. how can I apply the Pareto 80-20 principle; see Tactic #2 'Fire Your Worst Customers!')?
- How can I contribute to finding new ways for my business to create more Value for our customers?

Now leave your desk and ask your employees the same questions. Compare your guestimate with the reality. You might be amazed with the results.

What are your answers? Needless to say, **if your employees' answers are not in line with yours, you had better spend time with them explaining what the company is all about.**

Is the Purpose clear to you, as the owner of the business?

The first deal my consulting firm closed was the sale of my father's company. He and a friend had 50-50 ownership of an import and distribution company for fishing items. The need to sell the company emerged because it became too complicated to manage. They had 100 employees, and half the market. When I did my due diligence on them to understand the business, I asked my father and his partner what their Strategy was. Neither of them knew. They didn't even know what Strategy meant! So I asked them: 'You sell fishing items. If tomorrow there was an opportunity to make loads of money by selling bikinis, would you sell bikinis?' One said 'yes', the other said 'no'. So not only did they not have a Strategy, they also didn't know what they wanted from this company. Imagine what the employees knew or thought about the company's Purpose...

TAKE ACTION NOW!

Write down 5 ideas you will implement in the next 30 days that will make it clearer to everyone in the company how your business creates Value for its customers.

1. ______________________________

____

____

2. ______________________________

____

____

3. ______________________________

____

____

4. ______________________________

____

____

5. ______________________________

____

____

Tactic #50

Implement a Massive Action Plan

Set Goals and Actions in those areas important for your business's growth.

Massive Action Plan (MAP) is, as the term suggests, about planning massive action. You start with your Vision and with the End Goal. What do you want to achieve in a year or in a three-year period? Based on your overall Vision, get your first year Goal. Decide which areas of your business you will be working on to achieve your Goal. For each area you need to set Specific Goals, and break them down into quarterly Goals. Then, assign responsibilities to your team and get on with things.

When you develop your MAP consider the following:

1. **Vision.** This is where you see your company getting to in the long term.
2. **Purpose.** State clearly why you are doing what you are doing (see Tactic #49 'Ensure Your Employees Know Your Company's Purpose'). Why does your team want to be involved? Their Purpose should be included in your MAP.
3. **Consequences.** Include what happens if you fail to achieve the Objectives. Some people are Motivated by pleasure (the Goal), others are Motivated by pain (avoiding failure). Include both elements to Motivate your entire team.
4. **Goals.** Do the high-level planning with your senior staff. Select the areas you want to work on during the year, and set Goals for each area. Then set quarterly Goals for each area. Ensure that the person in charge of each area you choose to work on takes part in these discussions.
5. **Activities.** This is the 'what', 'whom' and 'by when': specific activities undertaken by specific members of your team, to be done by certain deadlines. Work on each area separately, and involve as many of your staff as possible in MAP-ing the area that is of concern to them.

Break down your Main Goals into Smaller Goals and then into digestible activities.

Do it like this!

Let's assume that as the business owner, your overall Goal is to increase profits by 50% within a year. You need to identify how you can achieve this Goal. Areas that you may want to consider are:

- *Sales. You want to increase Sales by 50%.*
- *Internal operations. You want to be more efficient internally, and decrease costs by 10%.*
- *Motivation of employees. You want to increase Motivation of your staff, so they are more efficient and produce better results. Let's say you want to increase the level of performance by 10%.*
- *Financing. You need to finance the growth. If you grow your Sales by 50% you may need to stock up on raw materials, or products, or even extend customer credit. So let's say you need additional finance amounting to 20% of your turnover.*

The above are the areas you need to focus on, and each area has its own Objective. In your MAP, you break Goals for each area into quarterly Goals. And then you set actions to achieve the quarterly Goals.

Let's look at Sales growth, the first area you want to work on. Your first quarter Goal is to establish the System you use to approach more customers. Your sales manager should be part of this discussion. Activities or solutions might include setting up a Partnership for new distribution channels, or simply organizing your internal sales team to be more efficient.

Let's say you agree to prioritize the latter. A simple way of increasing the efficiency of your sales staff is to remove their other responsibilities and allow them to sell only. If they are spending 40% of their time on preparing contracts, issuing invoices or drawing up other post-sale documents, this is 40% less efficiency in Sales. In other words, they only work at 60% efficiency. Once you have removed their admin work, they can spend 40% more time on Sales – and you should see a 40% increase in Sales. How do you remove the admin work from the salespeople? You simply employ another admin person to deal with Sales-related admin / paperwork.

When you then set up the Sales actions you may want to invite your entire sales team to contribute. They may bring New Ideas or approaches. And even if they don't bring any brilliant idea, you still want them involved, as you want them to take ownership of the plan, and be really focused on implementing it.

Have your relevant staff contribute to drafting their share of the MAP, rather than simply communicating it to them.

TAKE ACTION NOW!

Write down your overall one-year Goal, the reason you want to achieve this Goal, and what happens if you don't achieve it.

Goal: ______________________________

Reason: ______________________________

Consequence: ______________________________

Write down the areas you will be working on to achieve your Goal for next year:

1. ______________________________
____
____

2. ______________________________
____
____

3. ______________________________
____
____

4. ______________________________
____
____

5. ______________________________
____
____

Tactic #51

Share Short-Term and Medium-Term Goals with Everyone in the Company

You have a Vision for your company. You know where you want to get to. You may also know how to get there. But do your employees know?

Get your relevant staff involved when you plan each Area of Focus.

We already saw the value of internal communication in Tactic #48 'Ensure Your Employees Know What the Company Expects of Them'. Now, it is your turn to communicate Goals by setting Specific Objectives based on your Vision – and as you set them in your MAP in Tactic #50 'Implement a Massive Action Plan'. Starting with the aim or Vision in mind, go backwards, and set Specific Objectives for each quarter, based on the yearly Objectives. (For tips on setting these Objectives, see Tactic #52 'Use SMART Objectives…').

Next, assign tasks and responsibilities to people based on this medium- to long-term view. Regardless of how well organized you are and how clearly you have set your short-term and medium-term Objectives, you have to communicate these to your team – in particular to your managers, who should then communicate with their team members. Your managers should also set their own short- and medium-term Objectives, which should then be reflected in their team's everyday activities. Of course, Objectives have to be relevant to the employee's skill-set and the company's Vision.

You will achieve best results when your staff feels they are part of the business's Vision.

By establishing medium- and short-term Priorities in line with the overall business Strategy and Vision, you give your staff an overall understanding, a clear direction and a Purpose for their day-to-day efforts. In essence, you are facilitating *Goal Alignment*, which is critical for business success. This ensures that each person within your organization can see the direction for the business and knows how their job fits in the 'big picture'.

By allowing managers to access and view the Goals of other departments,

your organization can greatly reduce redundancy while finding better ways to support each other. With everyone working together toward the same Objectives, your company will execute its Strategy faster, with more flexibility and adaptability. Essentially, Goal Alignment strengthens your leadership and creates organizational agility by allowing managers to:

- achieve what is important, by focusing employees' efforts on your company's most important Goals;
- execute and deliver quickly, by understanding clearly responsibilities associated with Specific Goals;
- increase Accountability by assigning measurable, articulated Goals visible within the entire company.

Seeing the bigger picture!

One construction worker can think that he is digging a hole in the ground, while another knows that he is contributing to laying the foundation of the greatest highway on Earth. The work is the same, the mindset entirely different. Sharing with your team your current road map to making your Vision real helps your employees see the larger picture and understand the connection between their everyday chores and the final destination.

As a business owner, it is your responsibility to ensure your team leaders, managers and coordinators understand the difference between drilling a hole and laying the foundation for a great piece of work. It is also up to you to ensure that your leadership team is able to make people feel that they are part of colossal projects rather than simply overwhelm them with demanding and meaningless tasks.

TAKE ACTION NOW!

Write down your overall Goal:

____

____

____

Write down your Mini-goals. Once these are clear to you, involve your team to ensure these Goals are clear in their minds too. By doing this, they see how their tasks are linked to the business's Goals.

1. ______________________________________

____

____

2. ______________________________________

____

____

3. ______________________________________

____

____

4. ______________________________________

____

____

5. ______________________________________

____

____

Tactic #52

Set SMART Objectives…

...and be smart enough to know that no matter how SMART your Objectives, they might require reconsideration.

We have discussed that you set Goals in your MAP. Those Goals are in fact translated into Objectives, which you have to ensure are S-M-A-R-T. If you don't already know it, here is the S-M-A-R-T framework:

- **Specific:** Well-defined to inform employees exactly what is expected, when, and how much. With Specific Goals, managers can easily measure progress toward Goal completion.
- **Measurable:** Provide milestones to track progress and Motivate employees toward achievement.
- **Attainable:** Success needs to be achievable with effort by an average employee, not too high or too low.
- **Relevant:** Focus on the greatest impact to the overall company Strategy.
- **Time-bound:** Establish enough time to achieve the Goal, but not too much time to undermine performance. Goals without deadlines tend to be overtaken by day-to-day crises.

And most importantly, hold people Accountable for achieving the Goals. The easiest way to accomplish this is by involving them in the setting up their own Goals and Objectives. Every time you embark on a new project or a new initiative, go through the S-M-A-R-T process to clarify the Objectives, based on the over-riding Goals. The clearer this is for everybody, the higher the chances of the Goal being achieved. Those who are not involved in setting the direction in your company, should at the very least be informed about your Goals and their Objectives. Use this framework at the highest level, as well as for small projects. If you are about to launch a new product, this should be planned within the S-M-A-R-T framework too.

Some SMART and not so SMART Objectives

SMART Objectives	*Objectives that are not SMART*
Complete at least 25 cold calls to qualified prospects by September 1, 2010.	*Conduct as many Sales calls as possible as soon as possible.*
Increase Sales of Waffle Wraps to chain grocery stores by 8% over last year by December 31, 2010.	*Sell as many Waffle Wraps as possible this year.*
Convert 33% of leads to customers within 30 days of initial contract.	*Convert some leads every day so that you always have new customers.*
Follow up with every prospect and customer within 48 hours of Sales call.	*Follow up with every prospect and customers after a Sales call.*

To help set Specific Objectives ask yourself and your team:

- What are we going to do, with whom or for whom?
- How will this be done and what strategies will be used?
- Why is this important to do?
- Is the Objective understood?
- Is the Objective described with action verbs?
- Who is going to be responsible for what and do we need anyone else to be involved?
- Where this will happen?
- When do we want this to be completed?
- What needs to happen?
- Is the outcome clear?
- Will this Objective lead to desired results?

TAKE ACTION NOW!

Write down 5 S-M-A-R-T Objectives for your business:

1. ____
____
____

2. ____
____
____

3. ____
____
____

4. ____
____
____

5. ____
____
____

Tactic #53

Train Your Sales Staff Exceptionally Well

Top Training leads to better Skills and – equally importantly – higher Motivation.

As the business owner, you probably sold your product or offering initially yourself – or you are still doing so. You, or someone else, must have mastered such Sales, or your business wouldn't exist. You need that Knowledge to be transferred to your sales force and you (or whoever else performed the initial Sales) need to Train your current sales force. **It is not enough to tell them what to do. You need to show them how to do it. It is best if you can demonstrate to each of your salespeople how to do it.** Give them the process and tools they need to follow for the Sales, whether the steps to take, or a pitch or presentation style, or other materials they may need. Answer all their questions. Go into the field with them and check how they are doing. Observe and help them improve. You are their coach, so it is entirely your responsibility to Train them and to ensure they know what they are doing.

Record your Training sessions. You can use these recordings again with them in future, or with new recruits. Other people within your company will eventually use these recordings too.

There is never 'too much Training'! Perform frequent Training! As their coach, you need to have regular meetings with them, to constantly improve what they do. Observe what the Best Performers do, and get the others to follow suit. Of course, you can use outside Trainers, if you prefer, but make a point of getting involved too.

And if you don't know how to do it…

Get all your sales people together, look at the Best Performer and ask him to explain to the team what he does and how he does it, so the others copy what works for him. You are the facilitator, if nothing else. You need to ensure that step-by-step actions are being taught by your Best Performer(s).

Train your sales force and you will earn their loyalty.

TAKE ACTION NOW!

Write down 5 ideas you will implement in the next 30 days to Train your staff better, as well as to improve your company's Training System.

1. ______________________________

2. ______________________________

3. ______________________________

4. ______________________________

5. ______________________________

Tactic #54

Regularly Monitor the Motivation of Your Staff

Keep in touch with how your people perform and how engaged they are. Being aware is the minimum you can do.

The success of your business is highly dependent on the performance of your staff. And their performance is dependent on their Motivation.

As a small business owner, you don't really need complicated KPIs and sophisticated Performance Management Systems to know who is delivering and who isn't. Nor do you need cutting-edge Employee Engagement Surveys to ascertain how excited your staff is to work for you. Just go out there and see for yourself. Track Employee Motivation through observation of how enthusiastic they are about arriving at work, interacting with colleagues and engaging in activities to which they are assigned. You may also like to teach your managers to note everyone's reactions when undertaking a new project.

Keeping people engaged is most often as simple as eliminating certain tasks and removing their pain, rather than performing miracles.

I take time to talk regularly to each of my employees. (Granted, I don't have hundreds of them – yet.) I do this because I want to know how they feel about working with the company, what they like, what they don't like, what they expect, and where they see themselves. Such discussions help me paint a picture of the company that I can't see by myself. These talks also help make my organization more efficient as many of the best suggestions come from my staff.

Now we're talking!

When I was still testing Business Lens™ (our toolkit to identify what you don't do well or enough of in your business), I had everyone in the company fill in the survey (a series of multiple choice questions). I then had the results centralized into an Excel file, with one column showing the grades of each employee, though I did not know which grades belonged to whom. I noticed that most of the grades were in line with my expectations and relatively close one to another – except for one, which was way below the others. I knew immediately whom these grades belonged to: a colleague who was often moaning and complaining. His internal unhappiness was reflected in those grades, and in the distance between himself and the rest of the team. He wasn't happy

with us anymore, so he saw everything in a negative light. That same employee had produced great results for us in the past, but he simply wasn't motivated any more to work with us. Doing an exercise like this can help you spot those employees who have problems in or with your company, or it can confirm something you had suspected.

The fact that an employee isn't performing according to your expectations may not be his problem, but yours. Every time you are tempted to let someone go, use it as an opportunity to look in the mirror and learn. Somehow you either hired or promoted someone who failed to perform according to expectations. Ask yourself: how did this happen and how can I keep it from happening again? Be careful also to distinguish between valuable employees who are simply being misused or are misplaced, and those employees who are detrimental to your business's health, as a result of poor work ethic, apathy or overall lack of interest.

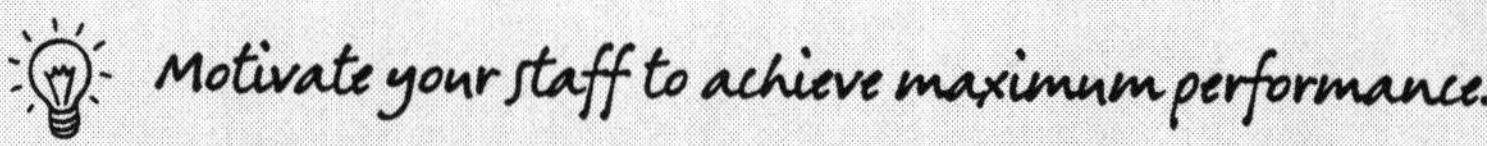

Maintaining appropriate levels of Motivation, satisfaction and performance among your work force is an on-going process. Don't let measuring employee sentiments be a one-time activity. Add it to your list of annual tasks through which you demonstrate to employees that you are genuinely concerned about their work life.

TAKE ACTION NOW!

Write down 5 ideas you will implement in the next 30 days to ensure you monitor and increase the Motivation of your staff:

1. ____

2. ____

3. ____

4. ____

5. ____

Tactic #55

Align the Individual Goals of Your Staff with Company Goals

...and be smart enough to know that no matter how SMART your Objectives, they might require reconsideration.

Try to accommodate your staff's wishes where possible. An employee might want to leave the office at 3 pm on Fridays and be happy to make up for this by putting in an extra hour per day from Monday to Thursday. Why not give this to her? Ask your employees what they want… and you will be surprised by what you hear! Often they don't want the things you think they do (like tons of extra money or fancy perks).

When I did the Massive Action Plan (MAP) for my company, I had my whole team contribute. One of the directions in the MAP was Tooliers®. When we filled in the Purpose (i.e. why we want Tooliers® to be a success), I was amazed to discover that my reasons were different from those of my team. There is a clear overlap, but some people have strong reasons centered on things like developing themselves, showing the world what we can do, helping lots of other small businesses do better business… the list goes on. Money was not the main driver for any of my staff!

How can you find out your employees' Goals? You ask them. Some don't have any, or simply haven't thought of their Goals and many may require more time to reflect on it – don't rush them. They need to understand what they really want. They also need to know what they want from your company. It can help to ask them the following question: 'Imagine you are walking along the street when a genie crosses your path. He asks you to tell him three wishes and promises to make them come true. What are those wishes?', Don't promise to fulfill them! Use this game to understand where your staff are coming from, and to meet them there, where possible and in a realistic way.

Now we're talking!

At some point I was in a rush to finish ***Business Lens™****, which was down to one person to finish. When I asked her to give it to me to finalize, so that we could send it to the programmers within the deadline, she told me she would prefer to do overtime and finish it. She wanted feel that she had accomplished something. I am very grateful she told me this. Of course I let her complete the job, even though it might have been* *quicker had I finished it myself. I gave her what she wanted and she felt good about her achievement. Plus, I could use that time to work on something else.*

Happy employees are more engaged and loyal and more productive in the short, medium and long term. **Investing in your staff's happiness by taking the time to know them and by getting them involved in the right projects pays off (literally).** Just think about all the recruiting, training and integration costs you avoid by keeping and developing your existing taskforce.

TAKE ACTION NOW!

Ask your staff what their Goals are and why they are working for your company. Write down 5 of these Goals and reasons and how you will try to fulfill those that are reasonable.

1. ____

____

____

2. ____

____

____

3. ____

____

____

4. ____

____

____

5. ____

____

____

Tactic #56

Don't Use Money to Motivate Your Staff

Say 'John, you have done a great job today' and watch his Motivation increase.

Pay your staff fairly, no question about it, but don't use money as the sole Motivation for your employees to perform. Money is there to ensure the comfort of your employees, but Motivation is obtained mainly through non-monetary means.

People like to be treated fairly and, from time to time, it is a good idea to give them more than that. Giving the royal treatment always works like a charm to rally people around your mission. The trouble is everyone has her own idea about what the royal treatment constitutes and, too often, the manager's idea of this is quite different from that of her employee. Never make the mistake of assuming that a raise or a bonus will do the trick for everyone. In fact, it can be difficult to know what makes certain employees tick. Some might react positively to having more freedom and enjoying flexible working hours. Others might be more excited about being publicly praised. Many would appreciate it and give more to their employers if the company would make their lives as working parents easier.

Just because you are driven by a dream of becoming a millionaire, or a billionaire, doesn't mean that your employees share that dream. The magic solution here is that there is no magic solution. **You have to listen, observe, bear in mind individual differences and then be sure to give people what makes them tick.**

Some ideas to implement and increase Motivation

- *Give your employees tremendous freedom, such as planning their week as they consider effective or trying their ideas for new products or simply trying new ways of doing things.*
- *Apply flexible working hours, flexible start and end times.*
- *Consider what each member of your team likes and is good at when you divide responsibilities.*
- *Offer 'concierge' services to your employees, whereby you contract someone to do personal jobs like taking clothes to the dry-cleaners, picking up a parcel, or even driving their kids to school.*

- *Give performance recognition in public (you and other managers). Make a habit of praising one employee every day!*
- *Have easy, regular conversations with your people.*
- *Show a natural interest in people.*
- *Say 'thank you' and give praise regularly.*
- *Give credit where it is due.*
- *Treat everyone equally and fairly.*
- *Always keep the promises you make – or don't make them.*
- *Delegate responsibility wherever you can, with guidance.*
- *Challenge your employees.*
- *Coach, support and guide your staff to their success.*

Still not convinced? Do you know it costs three times the salary of an existing employee to replace that employee? Think about the time it takes to find and recruit a new employee and the cost of training that employee to the same level of productivity. All the more reason to find out what Motivates your employees…

TAKE ACTION NOW!

Write down 5 cost-free ideas you will implement in the next 30 days to Motivate your staff:

1. ______________________________

2. ______________________________

3. ______________________________

4. ______________________________

5. ______________________________

Chapter 6
More for You, the Leader

Tactic #57

Work ON Your Business and Not IN The Business

Take that leap of faith! Trust your people, Delegate more, and earn yourself valuable time to deal with the strategic aspects of your business.

Let go! Yes, relinquish control. You may say, 'But this is my business! How can I let go?' Sure, this is your business, and you took it to the point where you are in charge and can control it. If you want to get to the next level, you need to accept you can't control everything anymore; you have to rely on and trust others in your team. People are happy to take more responsibility, and it's up to you to select the right person for that extra responsibility. That person will grow together with your business. She will assume more duties, she will learn more, she will be happier. As will you.

Now we're talking!

A few years ago I said to one of my colleagues: 'As of today, you are in charge of this division. If you have problems, come to me. But I believe you will manage to solve them yourself.' She was in shock initially, as she had not been expecting it. But guess what? She is still managing that division today and clients are happier than I could have made them. Why? Because she is totally focused on that division, which is something that I, as the business owner, would never have been able to do. I have too many other things to deal with!

Now that you have moved the heavier responsibilities to your team members, you are free to think. Indeed, you can stop and think. Imagine you are an angel flying above your business, looking down on what is happening there. Do you like what you see? Do you see a money-making machine or an ant's nest, with loads of ants running around, very busy, carrying food, making the nest, but not producing anything for you? Now that you have time, you have every reason to start applying the tactics in this book and to take your company to the next level.

TAKE ACTION NOW!

Write down 5 ideas you will implement in the next 30 days to better empower your staff so that you can Delegate and free up more of your time.

1. ______________________________

2. ______________________________

3. ______________________________

4. ______________________________

5. ______________________________

Tactic #58

Define Your Purpose

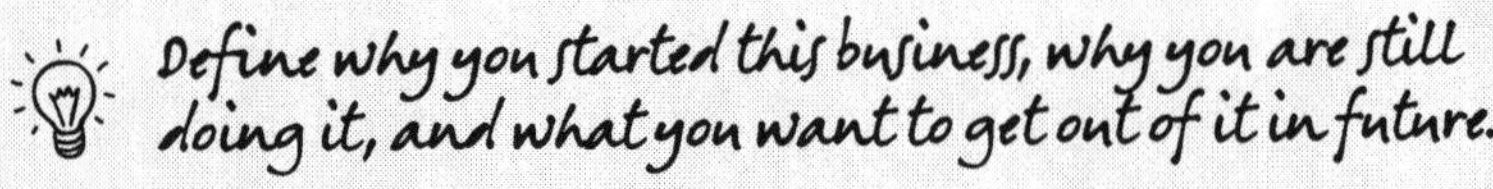

You created this company. Your company follows your personality, your drive, your Vision. By knowing where you are and what you want out of it, you will have more clarity on your business. You will be able to define your company's short-term and long-term Strategies, as well as the way you want the company to operate and function.

Maybe you created this business so you could travel the world and stay in in five-star hotels. So, besides profits, you want the company to operate without you having to be in the office all the time. That means your team has to function whether you are there or not. Either you have trusted people that you rely on, or you manage it remotely. And yes, of course it is possible to manage from elsewhere! Look at me: I am writing this book in Brussels, my staff is in Romania, my clients are in the U.S. and the operating company is in the UK. That's because I set up the business in this way to fit my lifestyle.

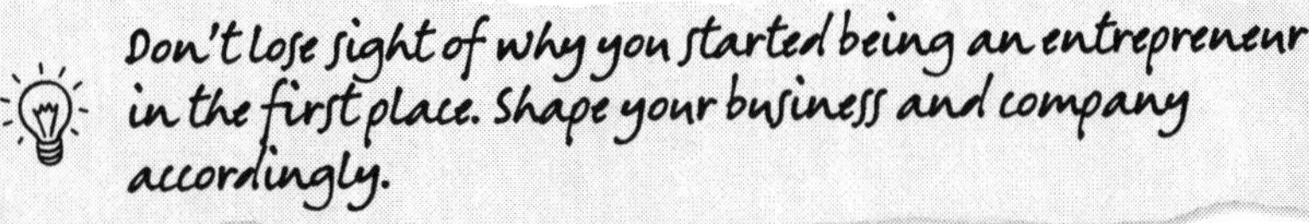

What are (or were) your real reasons for starting this business? For example, beyond profits and lifestyle, I have reasons like: helping small business owners work smarter; helping people stop repeating the same mistakes; creating Value for business people by showing them how to get out of the vicious circle of working in the business and not achieving the results they want. I also want to have fun! And I love learning new things every day. I want more challenges. I want to reshape the consulting industry, and push for really high-value professional services. I am tired of seeing mediocre advice provided by so-called Experts. I want to see more Value for small businesses and I want to see our clients become big and compete on equal footing with multinational companies.

TAKE ACTION NOW!

What is your Purpose? Write down why you started this business:

____

____

____

Write down 3 reasons why you are still in this business:

1. ____

____

____

2. ____

____

____

3. ____

____

____

Tactic #59

Brand Yourself

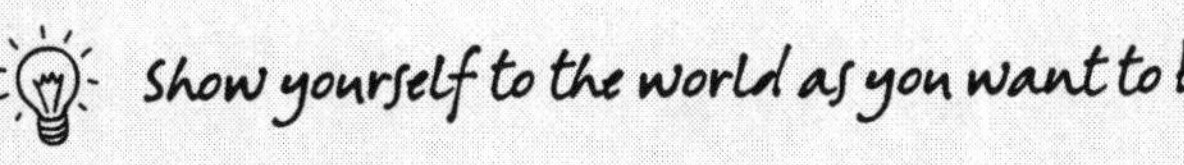

Who are you? What do you want people to know about you? How do you want people to remember you?

People like to do business with Experts. Identify your niche of expertise and position yourself as the Expert. If you are selling outdoor sports equipment, you need to know everything about such equipment. You are probably a sporty person who uses a lot of this equipment, in which case you also want to be known as the person who climbed the Himalayas or skied at an altitude of 4,000 meters.

I have decided that I want to become the world's top Small Business Growth Expert. Whenever a business owner has a Challenge, I want someone to recommend that she contact me. For this purpose, I have started speaking at conferences and within business communities. I am always happy to share my knowledge and expertise in large groups of entrepreneurs. I have created a Mastermind Group for Small Business Growth and Success on Google, where I provide daily advice (for free) to small business owners who post their Challenges. I have written a book: Shortcut to Business Success (www.ShortcutToBusinessSuccess.com); I have created two concepts for success in business (www.SecretToSuccessfullBusiness.com and www.SecretToEffectiveTimeManagement.com); and I have set up a foundation to help young entrepreneurs be successful in business (www.grupia.org/en).

But I also want people to know me, beyond the businessperson. This is why, on my Google+ profile, you will see this: Dived in the Amazon, visited six continents, skied at an altitude of 3,500 m, drove 250 km/hour on national roads and holds a yacht license.

Create and carefully manage your Personal Brand. You want everyone to see the best of you. Your Brand is what people say about you, especially when you are not around. These days, most people will Google you if they are going to meet you or have just met you. Ensure the 'Googleable you' is what you want to show.

Use online publicity to strengthen your Personal Brand

- *Create comprehensive profiles on Facebook, Google+ and LinkedIn, including a summary. See how I built my LinkedIn profile: uk.linkedin.com/in/ozanagiusca/.*
- *Write articles and have as many interviews published in the press as you can. Encourage people to write about you. Publish pictures of yourself online, especially in your social media profiles, so people recognize you.*
- *Use your Facebook page to associate your Personal and Professional Brand with the image of the people you hold in the highest esteem. Share your photos if you attend their training workshops, or meet them at conferences or events. Post about entering into a new Partnership. Post about your accomplishments. These will send powerful messages to your followers about your Personal Brand.*

With the rise of social media the days of hiding behind an impersonal website are long gone.

Make sure you are balanced and subtle about promoting yourself. You don't want to alienate people (or lose real friends because you're so busy using your social media profiles to promote yourself to clients). And depending on your industry or majority market it may not help to come across as full of yourself. In some countries and cultures, blowing your own horn is seen as admirable; in others it is viewed as shameless self-promotion. Adapt to your market.

Learn from the best. Check out the social network profiles of your idols. I get my inspiration from Tony Robbins (how did you know?), Richard Branson, Guy Kawasaki and others I admire and I can learn from.

TAKE ACTION NOW!

Write down 5 ideas you will implement in the next 30 days to build the Brand you want for yourself, or to strengthen your existing Brand:

1. ______________________________

2. ______________________________

3. ______________________________

4. ______________________________

5. ______________________________

Tactic #60

Create Networks

Tell me who your Facebook friends are, and I will tell you who you are.

Network! Constantly meet more people, learn about more people, express an honest interest in others, and you will see the benefits. Serve people! Be of real help, without expecting anything in return. The return will come when you need it.

The more people you know, the more access to information and other people you will have. Of course, this depends on the quality of the people you mix with. Seek to meet interesting people. You may learn something you wouldn't have known otherwise and that might be beneficial for your business. You may meet a new client or business partner. You may get an idea that, once implemented in your business, generates 30% more profits.

Go to relevant events. Identify where people you are interested in go and what events they attend and join the party!

Whenever you meet new people, learn about them, about their challenges, their aspirations. Help them with an idea, a piece of advice, an introduction. Share what you know and what can help them. You have a new trick to advertise for free using Facebook? Share it with other business owners. Don't worry that they will steal your idea. There is plenty of room for you and your Competitor to apply the same tactic. You want the person to remember that she got a really good tip from you. This is how you can build your brand and Relationships.

It's not necessarily who you meet, it's the access you get by meeting that person.

Apply it now!

At the National Achievers Congress in October 2013, I took a course on Business Growth (the Rainmaker Summit by Bill Walsh) in Las Vegas. While there I met a few people who have since been helping me with Tooliers®. And via these people, I am meeting more interesting people.

Whomever you choose to spend time with will determine who you become.

TAKE ACTION NOW!

Write down 5 actions you will undertake in the next 30 days to ensure you meet the people you want to meet, and build Relationships with them.

1. ____

____

____

2. ____

____

____

3. ____

____

____

4. ____

____

____

5. ____

____

____

Tactic #61

Associate with People Who Are More Successful than You

'We are the average of the five people we spend the most time with.' (Jim Rohn)

Do business, socialize, develop friendships, or simply be around people who are more successful than you. When you are surrounded by people like this, you become more successful. You learn from these people; you might make deals with them; you may be part of their 'circle of trust' and meet other More Successful People; you have access to information you wouldn't otherwise have. In addition, you can 'borrow' from their brand in building yours.

Imagine you post a picture of yourself with Richard Branson on your Facebook page, or on your website. Don't you think people will be more interested in you? Don't you think you will be perceived as more successful? (Now don't go and use Photoshop to 'produce' that picture!)

'Don't fake it until you make it... act as if you belong.' (JT Foxx)

Make it work for you!

I met JT Foxx at the aforementioned National Achievers Congress. He presented on the same stage as business gurus like Robert Kiyosaki, Gerry Roberts and Andy Harrington. (Of course he makes a big fuss out of sharing the stage with these famous people.) Foxx positions himself as the World's #1 Business Coach. Due to his strong desire to make loads of money no matter what, he does a lot of smart and unconventional things. (Be discerning and judge for yourself before buying anything from him!) At the Congress, he pitched himself as being much more approachable than the other speakers and offered to pose with us for photos. The reason, of course, is that he wants us, the public, to make him a celebrity. He is far from what he says he is, but he is using the masses – us – to make him what he wants to be. Imagine 5,000 photos with him on Facebook within a week of this event. And other 5,000 the following week, after another event. And so on...

TAKE ACTION NOW!

Write down 5 ideas you will implement in the next 30 days to associate with More Successful People:

1. ____

2. ____

3. ____

4. ____

5. ____

Tactic #62

Allocate Your Time to What Is Really Important

Mastering time management is a key success factor for the busy entrepreneur.

Time is like money. If you control it, you can create a satisfactory and productive working environment. If you don't control it, you can end up spending your working life in an exhausting and depressing muddle.

Set times aside to spend with each division / team / project and do not spend more time than you have assigned. Trust your teams can do the job correctly! Empower them to take full responsibility for their activities.

Step back from deadline-based work and seek out new kinds of activities that help to set a clear direction for your organization. Get people focused on a common set of Objectives and inspire, achieving results through your people and their ideas.

You are the leader. You want to succeed – so you need to focus on a specific set of Priorities, not just a specific set of Skills. I see a lot of small business owners falling into the trap of believing that their primary value comes from the technical expertise they bring to their business. As a result, they find themselves doing work their subordinates should be doing, cancelling one-on-one meetings and staff meetings because of more 'urgent' Priorities, and grumbling that no one works as hard as they do or can do the work of their department as well as they can. If you are concerned with return on investment, cost and quality control, motivation and retention of key employees, doing the jobs of your employees is a dangerous trap.

Empower your team

*A lot of people read how-to blog posts, but they do nothing with the information. I realized that business owners want to improve what they do, but don't know how and where to start. With the Diagnosis on Tooliers®, they find out what they need to Focus on... but they still don't know how to approach it. So we decided to develop **Action Plans** for various business success Tactics, whereby we give business owners step-by-step actions to master each Tactic; i.e. rather than teaching them or giving them another blog post to read, we give them real actions that they can do by themselves or with their teams.*

I have many specialists in my company mastering various Tactics, but when I asked them to draw up the Action Plans they struggled to get beyond the blank sheet of paper in front of them. So I had two options: (i) to build all the Action Plans myself, or (ii) to empower them to do it. Which do you think I went for? The second, of course. We had team brainstorming sessions, in which they all generated ideas and also came to understand what and how to go about the task required of them. Within a month we had 10 Action Plans! How long would it have taken, and how long would I have spent on the task, if I'd tried to do it all myself?

Mastering time management is a key success factor for the busy entrepreneur.

In the example above, consider the results after one month:

ROTI = (me empowering my team to do the Action Plans)

$$\frac{\textbf{10 Action Plans}}{\textbf{2 + 20 hours invested}}$$

(2 hours for initial brainstorming session, and 2 hours per Action Plan)

vs.

ROTI = (me doing it all by myself)

$$\frac{\textbf{1 Action Plan}}{\textbf{1 month of my time}}$$

Besides, you deserve a good work-life balance. Did you set up this company to create a job for yourself, or to build a successful business? The business should work for you, and you shouldn't work in your business. With the right attitude to time management, and the right organization of your business, you can work as much or as little as you like. Just decide what's important for you and work upon this decision.

TAKE ACTION NOW!

Write down 3 Priorities – things that are (truly) important to you – and at least one step towards realizing each of them.

1. ____

____

____

2. ____

____

____

3. ____

____

____

Tactic #63

Understand Your Company's Financials

Financial Management sounds complicated but you can do the basics yourself.

If you can read a nutrition label or a baseball score, you can learn to read basic financial statements. If you can follow a recipe or apply for a loan, you can learn basic accounting. The basics aren't difficult and they aren't rocket science.

Ensure you periodically read the accounts. Use the information to understand your company's situation. You should know:

- What the numbers on the page mean
- How to calculate further ratios from the raw data
- What to do to improve results in future

You should be able to understand and track the current financial health of your business without solely relying on your accountant. Some basic financial analysis could include making comparisons of your actual financial performance with forecast targets, performance in past years, and industry averages (business benchmarks).

Understanding your figures, or Financial Literacy, is an essential skill for a successful business owner. It is important that you understand and can analyze the financial statements of your business so you can manage and control your finances and make decisions armed with facts, not just intuition.

Make it work for you!

When you are due to have guests for dinner, you decide what you want to serve to them, identify the ingredients required for the meal, see what's available in your fridge and cupboards, and then decide what to buy. Only then do you buy. If, instead, you go to the supermarket immediately and buy whatever you find there, you may return home and find some of the things you just bought were already in your own fridge or, even worse, realize you haven't bought everything you need to prepare the dinner.

Think of your accounts as your fridge. They can help you with your planning for further developments, but only if you use the information in there. If you fail to use the information, you may end up with not enough Resources for your next project, which could eventually mean bankruptcy.

TAKE ACTION NOW!

Write down 5 questions you would like to ask your accountant (or a friend who is good with numbers) to increase your Financial Literacy; i.e. your understanding of your financial information.

1. ______________________________

____

____

2. ______________________________

____

____

3. ______________________________

____

____

4. ______________________________

____

____

5. ______________________________

____

____

Tactic #64

Raise Your Standards

Go that extra mile: your success might be just one step out of your present comfort zone.

Raising Your Standards means that you will not stop where you are right now, but rather will move forward to the next level. Continue to challenge yourself, to ask more of yourself. Our current standards always seem normal and acceptable in the moment, but when we reach a new level, we look back to the old standards and think 'those were some dark days.'

Leaders set and raise standards. As a leader, take time to define high standards. Invariably, many leaders inherited rules from others, leading them to live their lives using someone else's game plan. If you'd like to improve, consider creating your own game plan.

Your life is a direct reflection of the standards you hold – both for yourself and for others. This is a nearly universal truth that applies to every aspect of your life. From your profession, to your appearance, your relationships and your finances – they're all governed by the standards you hold them to. Most of the time these standards are set unconsciously, either adapted from the environment or indoctrinated into you by your family, and your standards are usually set far lower than what you're able to achieve.

'Any time you sincerely want to make a change, the first thing you must do is to raise your standards. When people ask me what really changed my life eight years ago, I tell them that absolutely the most important thing was changing what I demanded of myself. I wrote down all the things I would no longer accept in my life, all the things I would no longer tolerate, and all the things that I aspired to becoming.'
(Tony Robbins)

You might think one way to check your standards is to compare yourself to other people, but this is a waste of time. You will do nothing but get stuck in mediocrity. If you compare yourself with those people who have it worse than you, you'll find that you are a king. And if you compare yourself with people who have much more than you, you'll think you're a beggar. But this information has no value.

I Raised My Standards!

Back in 1999, I had a good job, my own big apartment, a nice car, a loving boyfriend... and I decided to leave Romania and do an MBA in London. Everyone around me said I was nuts. Why leave a life in which I spend every weekend at the seaside, or in the mountains, with friends and loved ones? Why leave a comfortable life, a comfortable home, to spend a year living in a room as big as my kitchen, watching every penny I spend? Why? Because I wanted more. I knew I was capable of more, but I didn't know how at the time. So I took the risk: I invested all the cash I had (and more) into my MBA. I risked everything I had back in Romania and I had the best year of my life. I discovered a whole new universe, improved my skills dramatically and eventually became an inspiration for the same people that had doubted my plans.

Since leaving it all behind to do my MBA, I have made a point of constantly learning new things. I want bigger, better, more from myself, and from life. And it feels good! I also have high expectations of my team, my products, my company. Because my standards are so high, I hardly ever get complaints from our clients. We surpass their expectations. Many come back for repeat business and recommend us to others.

Your own standards have a great impact on what you do, and especially on the results you get.

TAKE ACTION NOW!

Write down 3 ideas to Raise Your Standards:

1. ____
____
____

2. ____
____
____

3. ____
____
____

Tactic #65

Change Your Limiting Beliefs

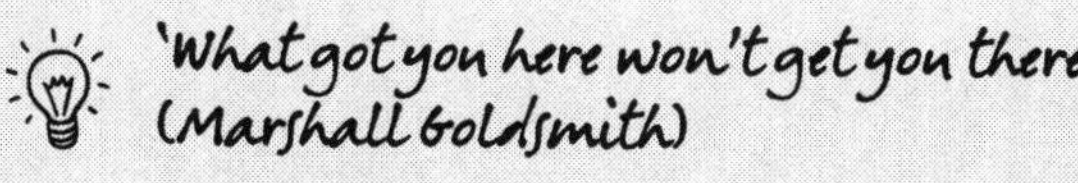

If you are an entrepreneur or a business founder / owner, you have probably come closer than most to the point of winning the battle against your Limiting Beliefs. You have already learnt that you have what it takes to do it on your own; after all, you gave up the safety of an 8-to-5 job for the thrill of pursuing your dream. You are already prepared to embrace change.

The strongest Limiting Beliefs of all – like 'it can't be done' – should have been eliminated from your vocabulary a long time ago. In all likelihood, you have learned to focus your mind and energy on how to do it rather than finding reasons not to do it or to procrastinate. You are already an inspiration for the people around you, as you are the living proof for them that 'we can't do it' is not your game.

You have to go even further though. In order to do this, you have to change any current Limiting Beliefs. **Your road to success is to constantly challenge your Limiting Beliefs. Keep an eye out for any self-limitations that might be sabotaging further success: it might be some behavior that pre-empts Innovation, some habit that triggers procrastination or inefficiency, something that reduces your profits.**

You hear a voice in your head saying, 'I'm not of the pedigree to get those special elite customers I've always wanted.' What is really going on behind this thought? Is this 'realism', modesty or just another Limiting Belief in disguise? Don't be modest or critical about yourself, just go out there and start chasing those Ideal Customers you want to serve. Even if you don't know, right now, how to create Value for them, you have what it takes to figure this out and to become their favorite provider.

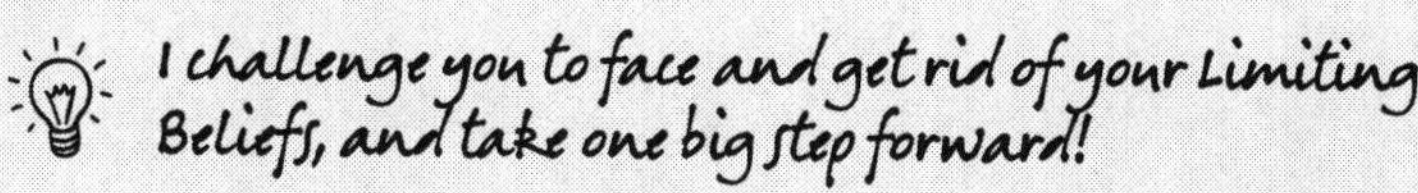

Learn the lesson!

Some years ago, my boyfriend suggested I start an online platform whereby companies for sale could be advertised to potential buyers. I said, 'No, I am a great consultant, I love what I am doing. Why change? Plus, there is a particular way to sell companies; they're not like shoes or books, which you can put online and off they go.' Guess what? Someone else has created such a platform – and I am building my own internet company. I had a Limiting Belief that stopped me from pursuing an opportunity.

TAKE ACTION NOW!

Write down 5 questions you would like to ask your accountant (or a friend who is good with numbers) to increase your Financial Literacy; i.e. your understanding of your financial information.

1. ____

2. ____

3. ____

4. ____

5. ____

Tactic #66

Model Others

Learn through Modeling to shortcut your road to success.

Learn by imitating or observing the behavior and actions of those you admire or want to emulate. **Modeling is a form of learning whereby individuals ascertain how to act or perform by observing another individual.** Most human behavior is learned in this manner: from observing others, we form an idea of how new behaviors are performed; on later occasions this coded information serves as a guide for action. Think back to when you were a child, or observe your own children now. One child climbs the tree, the others join in. One child has sunglasses, the others ask their parents for sunglasses too.

Advertising often exploits this concept to make us buy products or services. You watch a TV commercial that suggests drinking a certain beverage or using a particular hair shampoo will make you popular and win the admiration of attractive people. Sometimes you model the behavior and make the purchase.

You may have learned how to tell a joke better after watching Jay Leno's stand-up routine on TV. If you're at a party and feeling uncomfortable, you might learn how to act by watching how others are performing in the same situation. In business look at what More Successful People do, and imitate and adapt this for your own success. Learning from others is a shortcut to more rapid development, both of yourself and of your business.

Imitate and make your own improvements.

I imitate and I am proud of it…

A few months ago, a highly regarded business person in Romania suggested I talked to another highly regarded person. I initiated the meeting, and that person asked me who I was. Why should she meet with me? She is not on LinkedIn, nor is she 'internet literate', so all she could see was my bio on the website of my consulting company (i.e. just another consultant!). Frustrated with her response, I realized I needed to have my own website, to show the world who I am. So here I am working on my website… How do I do it? I

follow our Action Plan on Websites, of course! One step recommended there is to research other sites that have the same purpose as yours. So here I am again, looking at sites of other successful women, such as Shaa Wasmund, Marie Forleo and Joanna Martin. I take the idea of having a video teaser at the bottom of the page from one, of including pictures from my private life from another, and so on… Yep, this is what I mean by imitating: not copying the whole thing and just replacing the text or colors. You still need to be YOU! You need to be authentic. (And no, I am not the only one who does this. Most successful people do it to! Why reinvent the wheel, when you can just improve it?)

TAKE ACTION NOW!

Write down 5 people you admire, and whom you find do things better than you. For each person, write down what you really like about him / her. These are the qualities you want to start Modeling.

1. ______________________________
____
____

2. ______________________________
____
____

3. ______________________________
____
____

4. ______________________________
____
____

5. ______________________________
____
____

Tactic #67

Give MORE than What You Expect to Receive

Use this as a rule of thumb: give five times what you would like to receive. And sometimes, give merely for the sake of giving.

Simply offer with no expectations. I know you are not a charity, but gone are the days when you could charge for everything, from the first time you interacted with your customer. People are bombarded today with information, publicity, even free products. As a consequence, a lot of businesses have understood that they need to give a taste of their offering for free to attract customers (see, for example, Tactic #26 'Start a Relationship with Your Prospect').

What I am talking about here though is giving in general, not giving in order to attract more customers. **You want people to love you; you know by now that people prefer to do business with those they like. And how do you make others fall in love with you? By giving!**

When you give a present to your child or your mom, do you say, 'Hey, I spent $X on this. Remember that so you buy me something of equivalent value when my birthday comes'? Or do you enjoy the recipient's joy, which you created when you gave that present? Why not do the same in your business life? You can give to your employees, to your suppliers, to any partner.

Get giving! Here are some ideas:

- *Why not invite a possible recruit for lunch instead of organizing a traditional boardroom interview? It will make an impact on her, and even if you decide not to hire her, she will remember you, and will speak highly of you and your company.*
- *You just closed a good deal: why not take your team out for lunch, or even a weekend away! Celebrate with those who were involved, treat them. They will be grateful and more committed to working for you.*
- *A Good Employee leaves your company: take her out to lunch. You never know when you will need to exchange information about the latest trends in your industry, or if she will one day be running the sales department of your Competitors.*

TAKE ACTION NOW!

How could you Give More? Write down 5 things you could give, without expecting anything in return:

1. ____

2. ____

3. ____

4. ____

5. ____

Tactic #68

Add a Big Fat Zero to Your Ambitions

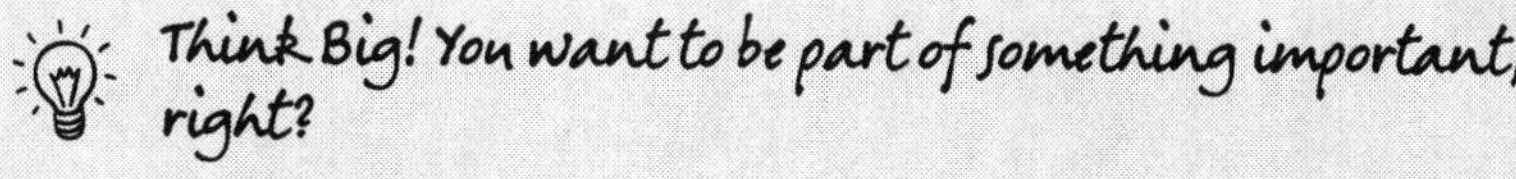

Significantly increase your ambitions. Yes, tenfold! And don't think it is impossible. Instead think: how can I make it happen? Most of the time, we do what we do and how we do it, because we have been programmed to do it this way. And we have also been programed to expect certain results.

Has your kid ever come up to you and asked for something outrageous? My son is only four years old and he wants an excavator. A real one! He doesn't think it is unachievable, or that it doesn't make any sense for him to have one. All he thinks is, 'How can I get it?' And you would be amazed by the ideas he tells me in order to get it! And you know what, he talks about it every day!

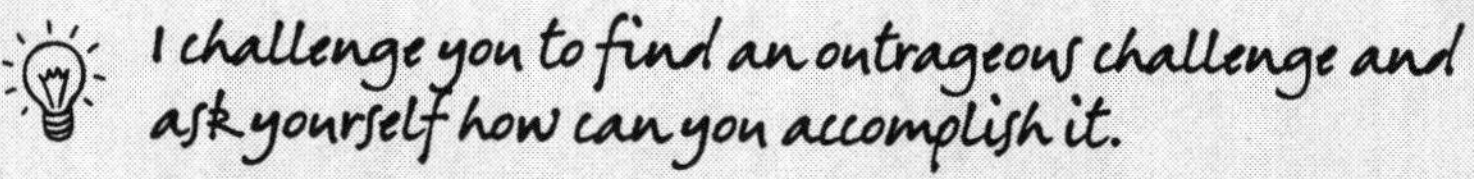

Once you think this way, **your mind will start coming up with ways of achieving it.**

Have you ever had a significant decrease in income? Let's say you are used to having an annual cash flow of $100,000. Something happens to your business, and you only net $10,000 for the year. What do you do? You do everything possible to get back to $100,000 – because this is YOUR number. It is what you are used to getting, what you expect. This is what you set your mind at. Try this in reverse: set your mind at $1,000,000 a year (for example); this is now YOUR number. If you are earning $100,000, you are earning only 10% of your Goal. So you know what you need to do!

Psssssst!

Do you want to know my number? It is $1,000,000,000 in Sales with Tooliers®. How does this sound to you considering that, as recently as 2008, I had no income and was $1,000,000 in debt? It may sound crazy to you, but is seems completely realistic to me! My mind is there, and I will achieve it. (Watch this space!) Of course this wasn't my target in 2008; the more we achieve, the larger the number or Goal becomes.

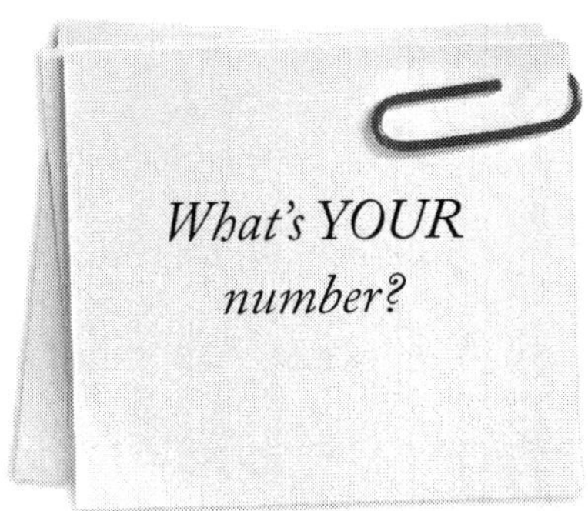

TAKE ACTION NOW!

What was your Goal before reading this chapter?

____

____

____

Now add a zero to it. In other words, make it 10 times bigger. Think Big! This is what you need to go after.

____

____

____

Tactic #69

Seek Breakthroughs in Your Business

A Breakthrough is any important development that may lead to major progress, change, or success. Pursue Breakthroughs! Don't wait for them to find you!

This is how it works!

Let's assume you drive a grey Ford F-150, which you bought last year. Before last year, how many grey Ford F-150s did you see in the streets? And how many do you see today? Would you agree that you see many more than you did before buying your car? Do you think there are more such cars around today than a year ago? Or do you see them because your awareness has been heightened after buying one?

Opportunities exist all around you. Open your eyes to see them!

To achieve Breakthroughs in your business, you need to start with yourself. Explore, discover, challenge, and grow to achieve Breakthroughs within. Become who you seek to be. **Become the best possible version of yourself.** Identify and release your true potential. Have a clear Vision, see the big picture, be strategic and creative. Start from the current reality and focus on the desired results, to finally reach the Vision. Have the courage to take sustained risk, confront tough areas, and have high expectations. Always think of serving others and creating Value. And don't forget your inner greatness: have substance, be true to your ethics and values, show integrity, and build trust.

TAKE ACTION NOW!

Over the next five days be more open and aware, and write down 5 New Ideas or New Opportunities you hadn't noticed before.

1. ____

2. ____

3. ____

4. ____

5. ____

Tactic #70

Invest in Yourself

 *Knowledge is power. It is yours to use for a lifetime.*

To me, the term 'investing in yourself' means continuously developing yourself as a person. (And no, I don't mean buy more clothes, that is investing in your wardrobe.) Invest in your own education in areas where you desire learning and growth. Take time off daily operations to read, to talk to people, to go to training sessions, conferences… to open up your horizon. You never know when or how the next big idea will come to you. Read biographies of successful people. No one can keep you from achieving your aspirations as long as you're willing to pursue your Goals and never give up.

Investing in your own Knowledge is risk free. I can't promise an exact return on investment, but it will always be positive. Become addicted to continuous improvement and increase your Knowledge consistently and constantly and, in time, you will become the person you wish to be. Then you will no longer have to chase after success – success will follow you. Your mind will become magnetized to attract success.

Knowledge is a powerful asset. The main difference between the general manager and the cleaning lady in a company is their Knowledge. The general manager knows something the cleaning lady doesn't. That is why he earns a hundred times more than she does. Many business people struggle because they just won't take the time to learn about accounting, marketing and all that goes with doing business. You do what you like doing – that's how you got to where you are. But if you want more, you need to learn more.

I think of my Knowledge as a collection. Whenever a client has a Challenge I pull out the relevant Knowledge and I provide the Solution. This is why people pay so much for my services – I have the Knowledge to solve their problems. I also constantly add to that Knowledge. I read something new or watch a webinar every day, I go to conferences and workshops. I invest time and money in my Knowledge because it gives me power. I use the latest marketing techniques firstly to market my product, but also for the benefit of our clients. They know they will get the freshest and best information; this is why they come to me.

Don't just do it every now and then; the trick is to include self-development activities in your daily routine. Adopt the self-development mindset by constantly looking for opportunities to learn more. The next level is to turn your entire business into a learning organization. Inspire others to invest in themselves, support others in their development and establish self-development support relationships across your company. Teach your people to Coach and Train each other. Avoid becoming overly self-sufficient, the "I know it all" boss. Aspire instead to becoming the inspirational leader of an organization open to learning and self-improvement.

Tonight, instead of watching a movie, watch a TED talk.

This is what we like to see!

You might think that once you know it all, you are done... Well, you may be surprised to learn that Tony Robbins, who trains millions of people every year, undertakes regular Training himself. Have you noticed the change in his voice over the past few years? Yep, he hired a voice coach. And did you know that, some years ago, Robbins had Chet Holmes (now deceased), author of The Ultimate Sales Machine, help him with his marketing and sales?

How many books does Robbins read? Probably more than any of us read! How many coaches does Robbins have? Again, probably more than any of us! If Robbins constantly seeks and absorbs Knowledge, we should do it too!

TAKE ACTION NOW!

Write down 5 actions you will undertake in the next 30 days to increase your Knowledge on a subject of your choice:

1. ____

____

____

2. ____

____

____

3. ____

____

____

4. ____

____

____

5. ____

____

____

Tactic #71

Open Yourself Up for Change

Great leaders are open to Change if they come across new information they had not considered. A successful leader is one who is undeterred with the changes around him, no matter how difficult they are. If it were easy, you would already have done it!

'Change is the law of life. And those who look only to the past or present are certain to miss the fortune.' (John F. Kennedy)

Here's why you need to apply this tactic!

When driving, if your route is blocked by road works, what do you do? You take an alternative route or face hitting a dead-end. Apply the same principle to your business. It's not as easy to do or accept and you may believe your way works – after all, you have done it so many times and might as well do it again – but don't allow yourself to get stuck in an approach that may no longer be appropriate. If you try to continue on the same road, despite the construction work, you will waste time and petrol while those who take an alternative route will get to the destination before you. You also risk missing the event you were trying to attend!

Of course the 'dead end' will not always be as obvious as in the example above. But it is your responsibility as the leader to anticipate Challenges and adapt accordingly in advance. The alternative route may not be clear to you, but you will discover it on the way. You may even have more fun on this route! As a leader you need to be open to changes in the environment and come up with ways to deal with them. As the saying goes: you cannot change the direction of the wind, but you can adjust the sails to reach your destination. Know how to steer the ship in the right direction.

If you want more money, less stress and some well-deserved recognition, you'll have to do things slightly different to achieve different results. Open yourself to Change to achieve what you want, to attain your future Goals.

If you are the kind of leader who believes you know it all (you have spent all your life in this industry and there is no other way…), you may be preventing New Ideas and New Perspectives from taking root. This is a dangerous

position to be in as you almost certainly kill any possibility for Innovation and will repeat the same mistakes.

TAKE ACTION NOW!

Write down 5 things you would like to change about yourself. Change yourself first and then your business will skyrocket.

1. ____

2. ____

3. ____

4. ____

5. ____

Chapter 7
Sustain Your Business Long-Term

Tactic #72

Determine Your Product's 'Buying Criteria'

Understand what influences your customers to buy products like yours so you proactively influence their decision and tip the balance in your favor.

Buying Criteria is a set of rules / algorithms / preferences that a prospect applies when making a purchasing decision; it is those factors that matter most to the buyer when choosing a product. If you are a woman you will easily understand this: remember your list with characteristics of your dream man? What you look for when you search for Mr Right? (And sorry guys, I hate to break it to you: Mrs Right will have to have a lot more than big boobs and blonde hair!)

Whenever someone buys something, they buy to satisfy a Need or to solve a problem. Every person has different criteria they apply when deciding on the Solution to their problem. These criteria include all the information required by the customer to make their buying decision. The answers to these questions help the customer to make an informed decision:

- What is it?
- Why should I buy it?
- What will I get?
- What is the price?
- Why do I even need it?
- Why should I buy it from this seller?
- What's the deal?

Each type of product or service will have different Buying Criteria. You need to really understand why people buy your product and what matters most to them. Examples of criteria could be: the look and feel, the credibility of the seller, the smell, the convenience, the price, the customer service etc. Please note that each person could have different Buying Criteria for each product in different situations. If it is hot outside and I want a cold drink or an ice cream, I will buy the one I find first (so Buying Criteria is convenience). But if I want drinks or ice cream for a party I organize at home, my Buying Criteria is price, so I go to a large supermarket.

Usually people are not Experts in the field of whatever they are buying; i.e. in whatever you sell. **By knowing and fulfilling their Buying Criteria, you can teach every buyer how to be a better buyer of your type of product or service.** If Häagen-Dazs tells me that their ice cream has half the calories of the lowest fat ice cream available in the street, I may wait and walk a bit further to get one of their ice creams; thanks to new information, my Buying Criteria shifts from convenience to health (or the least unhealthy!).

The Milkshake story

Harvard Business School professor Clay Christensen regularly uses this story to show his MBA students how important it is determine the 'job' your product does... A fast food chain wanted to increase its Sales of milkshakes. They undertook major research to understand why people were buying milkshakes, and what the real Competitor / Substitute was for milkshakes. You might think a soft drink, a fresh juice or a banana. However, the research revealed that most milkshake Sales were being done in the morning, to customers who had an hour commute to work and wanted something to kill the time and have something to do with their hands. A banana is too quick to consume; same for a juice. A milkshake fulfills this criterion perfectly: due to its thick consistency, it takes longer to consume and involves putting the hands to use more times and over a longer period of time.

Once you understand your customers' Buying Criteria, you have two options:

(i) Match the criteria as closely as possible

(ii) Influence them. (See Tactic #83 'Build Trust, Credibility and Respect' for more on this.)

TAKE ACTION NOW!

Write down 5 Criteria that people use when buying the type of product / service you provide:

1. ____
____
____

2. ____
____
____

3. ____
____
____

4. ____
____
____

5. ____
____
____

Tactic #73

Create Your X-Factor

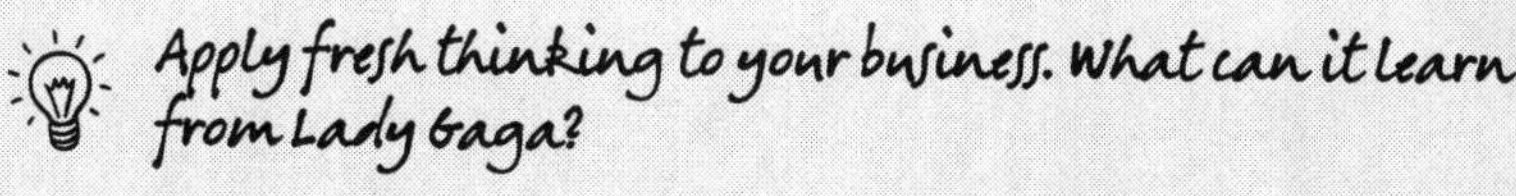

An X-Factor is the secret ingredient that helps you achieve your Objectives faster. It is what you do better than your Competitors – better than anybody else. It is your competitive edge. It is also your aura of authenticity. Find your company's X-Factor and put it to work for you.

Creating your X-Factor is using your company's unique Skills and Resources to implement strategies that your Competitors cannot implement as effectively. And yes, you are part of those unique Resources! Your company's X-Factor could be anything from successfully revamping a product or service to developing a new process; partnering with your worst Competitor to selling to customers you would never dream of reaching; from reorganizing around customers instead of products to 'productizing' your service.

Going back to college: I am sure you knew (or knew of) that girl who everyone wanted to go out with… she wasn't necessarily more attractive than any other girl, but she had this mysterious quality about her (which turned out to be her wicked sense of humor) and it meant guys were queuing to date her. Or the girl who, frankly, had terrible dress sense, but had guys wrapped around her little finger. Why? Her X-Factor was a kind of feminine fragility that men were attracted to, and her killer smile sealed the deal.

The X-Factor is your business's ability to add intangible Value – Value that goes beyond what anybody can measure with the usual tools. It is the ability to find a way to do more for your customers than anybody else does and to consistently maintain these high standards for fair prices.

There are likely to be plenty of businesses that do something similar to your business. However, no one does it exactly the way you do. This element is what differentiates you from the rest; it is your business's X-Factor. Your personality, your own X-Factor, is also clearly reflected in your business's X-Factor.

Know what your current X-Factor is, but also think about the future, and what your X-Factor should become. If something has never been done before, ask yourself why, and how you can use that to deliver more Value to your customers.

By finding your X-Factor, you find the advantage that puts you way ahead of Competitors in a key area like customer loyalty, pricing or employee retention. Your X-Factor can leave your rivals miles behind you and unable to catch up. The discovery of your X-Factor also provides you with the clarity and momentum to produce the best long-term results and build a truly awesome business. Once you find it, keep it as quiet as possible so that your Competitors don't get it! Failing to establish such a competitive edge puts your business in peril as it is then easy for others to sneak up from behind. The sooner you discover your X-Factor, the sooner doing business will become easier.

Learning from Lady Gaga

She can sing and play the piano, but it is how she 'shows up' that is totally unique to Lady Gaga. This is what has made her a Superstar. I am not suggesting pink hair or flesh suits; however, I am suggesting creating a style which is uniquely your own and represents who you are. Then, be consistent with it. This is how you 'show up' and how people will remember you. The entire customer experience you create is unique to you, and could be your X-Factor.

Think of companies you buy from, and ask yourself why you choose them. For example I love Starbucks – and I don't even drink coffee. My favorite drink is their caramel Frappuccino. I love the taste of this drink and have yet to find any drink that tastes as good. However, it is not just the Frappuccino I like about Starbucks. I love the coffee smell when I enter, the music, the overall atmosphere. It just makes me feel good when I am inside Starbucks. I have developed such a love for Starbucks that I miss it when I am in Brussels and will sometimes take a detour to pass by Gare Central to get my Frappuccino. In London, I always set up meetings in Starbucks. I know my way around London based on Starbucks. You get my point: they've got me. And they got me because of their carefully developed X-Factor. I can't tell you exactly what it is, but I know it is there.

TAKE ACTION NOW!

Write down 5 secret ingredients that will help you establish your business's X-Factor:

1. ____

2. ____

3. ____

4. ____

5. ____

Tactic #74

Use 'Core Story'

Tell Stories to communicate the advantages of your product while establishing a strong human connection with your customers.

In Tactic #11 'Tell Stories to Sell', we discussed the role Story can play in making your product personal and giving potential and existing customers a sense of ownership of the product. Developing a Story to tell your ***prospects*** will lead to a natural interest in buying your product. The Story should be able to create the Need for your product without you even mentioning it. The Story will also include ***Buying Criteria*** you fulfill, so it leads the buyer to choosing your product. Communicate your X-Factor (see previous tactic) in a way that is valuable to your audience.

The Core Story has to combine the power of data and research. In other words, include facts, statistics and numbers to prove your point. Facts alone, however, are not interesting. They have to be couched *within* a Story. Use more market data than product data to make your product or service appear more important. Market data is information generally valid about the market / population you are talking about, whereas product data is about a certain product or group of products. The more complex your product or service, the more data you need to use. This offers you the opportunity to appear as an Expert in your field.

Let's look at the Buying Pyramid below:

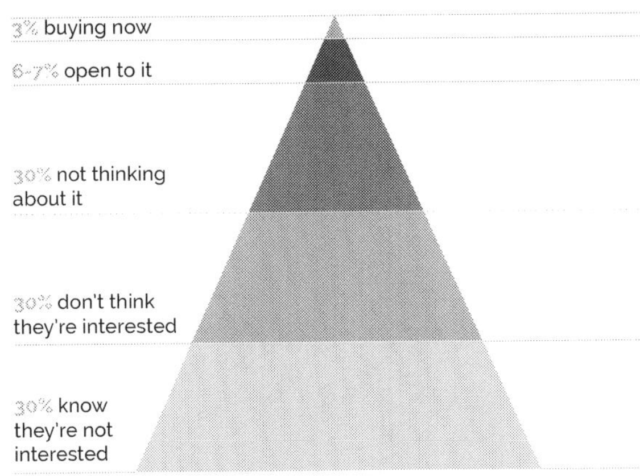

Source: Adapted from The Ultimate Sales Machine by Chet Holmes.

Only 3% of people are ready to buy a certain product at any given moment. Another 7% are open to buying it in future, and the rest are not even interested. For people to become more open to the product you sell, they need a Story. The main point of this Story is thus to have them be more interested, and convert them into the group that wants to buy now; i.e. you want to increase that segment beyond 3%. This way, you increase the demand for your product, and you attract more customers to buy your product. **As you include Buying Criteria in your Core Story, potential customers will naturally gravitate towards your product.**

As you include Buying Criteria in your Core Story, potential customers will naturally gravitate towards your product.

Help your potentials visualize how their life will become better after buying what you are promoting.

Here's how it's done!

Let's say you sell vitamins that help people live healthier and thus longer. Only 3% of the population is actively looking to buy vitamins. Your Core Story could be along these lines: Vitamins help people be healthy and live longer. Research proves that 90% of people taking vitamins live on average five years longer than those who do not take vitamins (market data). Vitamin X (yours) has ingredient Y, which helps the body's cells regenerate twice as quickly as the ingredients in other vitamins (product data).

TAKE ACTION NOW!

Write down 5 ideas you will incorporate in your Core Story:

1. ____
____
____

2. ____
____
____

3. ____
____
____

4. ____
____
____

5. ____
____
____

Tactic #75

Train Everyone in Your Company to Say Something Valuable about Your Company

Strategic communication is a fancy term for something quite simple: getting everyone (employees, customers, partners) used to saying something valuable about your company, products and services.

Encourage everybody in your company (you and your staff) to say something valuable about the company at every opportunity – no matter what the interaction is, no matter whom the interaction is with. You may want to have a meeting in which you explain to your staff how good it is for the company when they share what they like about working there. The staff could say what they are proud of, or mention aspects that resonate with them. If you get your staff excited about being in your company, this will come naturally to them.

The more people that spread the word about your company, the better – even if no immediate business comes from it, or if the audience currently has no Need for your product. **If people are impressed with what you and the others say about the company, they will remember you, and they will contact you when they do need the product you offer.** Moreover, they too will spread the word if what you and your employees say resonates with them.

Think back to your college days again… you hear various guys talking about a blonde girl with blue eyes who always wears short skirts that show her beautiful legs. Apparently she is not only pretty, but also smart. You know she's in class 7B, so you take a detour via class 7B, hoping you will see her. What happened here? You got information about this girl from various sources and, curious, you did something out of your way to see her. Don't you think your potential customers might do the same if they constantly hear positive comments about your company?

This is what we like to see!

My colleague Valeriu bumped into a former colleague in the street. They went for a coffee to catch up, and Vali told him about his life, which of course included his job. He mentioned, with passion, how good we are at helping business owners grow their companies and shared various stories about Happy Customers. By the end of their coffee, his former colleague asked him if we could help his company grow, as he had been struggling to do so for years.

Get your staff to spread information about the great elements of your business.

Anyone in the company can say something nice and of value about your company. The doorman might say: 'I love it there. Every morning, the two big bosses greet me with a smile and one brings me coffee every now and then!' This shows that the bosses care about their employees and the message transmitted by the doorman may have a positive impact when a potential future employee considers joining the company.

The doorman can be your promotional representative, spreading around nice messages about your company.

Here are some examples for inspiration:

- This is a great company. Not only do we offer top quality services to the client, but we the employees are also treated extremely well.
- We care for the environment; our company has a policy of saving energy
- For every $1,000 we make, we donate $1 to Save African Children Association, which feeds 3,000 children annually.

TAKE ACTION NOW!

Write down 5 ideas of valuable information that your team could say about your company, to help you spread the word on the good elements of your business. Once you have these ideas, make sure you Communicate them to your team and Train them to convey these qualities to others.

1. ____

____

____

2. ____

____

____

3. ____

____

____

4. ____

____

____

5. ____

____

____

Tactic #76

Communicate Your Ultimate Strategic Position

Hanging your mission statement on the wall doesn't do it anymore. Communicate the strategic positioning of your business, starting from your customer's side of the story.

Decide on your Ultimate Strategic Position (USP) – not to be confused with a Unique Selling Proposition – and make sure you and your staff communicate it all the time. The USP – the strategic positioning of your business – must always be top of mind. USP is what you want to be known for as a company, which is also part of the reason your customers purchase from you.

Your USP must be clear, and focused on what your customers get – not on what you offer; i.e. think of the benefits your customers receive first. For example, my USP for the company is: to become the premier platform where small business owners get the right affordable assistance to significantly grow their businesses and achieve the success they deserve, whilst investing the least time and money in growth'. This focuses on the customer. My USP is not 'we offer business growth services'.

Once you are clear on what you want to be known for, train your staff about your USP. Ensure they all communicate it, especially to your clients, prospects and business partners. Use any channel available: one-to-one discussions, PR, webinars, any marketing materials, videos, trade shows, to ensure your clients know what you want your company to be, and how you want to be perceived.

By highlighting the importance of your product and your company to your prospects (their benefits), you maximize the chances of selling. By having your customers and prospects perceive you as you want to be perceived, you attract more interest from the right customers, and will be the preferred choice when prospects are ready to buy the type of product you sell.

Once your USP is set and communicated, marketing it no longer becomes as big a deal. That's not to say you should forget all about marketing your product – just that your brand comes into its own and often experiences organic growth.

This is how it works!

In college I used to organize huge parties. I would easily get 100 people to attend a party at my flat, in the mountains, at the seaside or even a field in the middle of nowhere. People came to my parties because it was well known that the parties were fun and that beautiful people and the crème de la crème attended. Of course, at the time I didn't know anything about USP. I was just naturally throwing good parties, which people would talk about afterwards, and so the word would spread. I got to the point where I could tell just a few people when and where the party was, and 100 people would show up. I didn't have to do the hard work of calling them (this was before the internet and mobile phones!).

TAKE ACTION NOW!

Write down 5 key points that make up your Ultimate Strategic Position:

1. ____

2. ____

3. ____

4. ____

5. ____

Tactic #77

Help Your Customers Achieve More Success

Don't get obsessed with selling: focus on discovering new and better ways for your products and services to improve your customer's life, and Sales will flourish naturally.

Gone are the days when you sold a product or service in your first meeting with the client and then said goodbye. Buyers are more educated and have more information available to them these days. They expect to get value for money, no matter what they buy.

Building Relationships with customers, continuing to communicate, and solving customers' problems are tactics we all know about. Your Competitors are already doing these. **You need something that goes beyond and gives true benefits to your customer: you need to help your customer achieve more success.** This really means caring about your customer and doing everything possible to make him more successful. The more success you create for your customer, the more often he will return to you or recommend you to others.

Currently, sales professionals tend to focus on pushing their product and achieving their numbers. They do not care much about finding Solutions that exactly meet the Needs of their customers. The Buyer-seller Relationship is fundamentally broken. Let's face it, buyers don't trust sellers. They are tired of being sold to. The result for the sellers is often missed quotas and disloyal customers. This is unfortunate because, if you think about it, the buyer and the seller really do want the same thing: a Solution that meets the client's Needs.

You may think this tactic only applies to ***B2B***, or businesses that sell training, personal development or career advice, but you would be wrong. It applies to every business. Yes, even if you sell ice cream or operate a parking lot, you can help your customer achieve more success.

This is what we like to see!

When I was single in London, I used to go clubbing a lot. I particularly liked a new club called Elysium, on Regent Street. A month after it opened, I had a hot date. I really liked the guy and wanted to impress him. I arrived half an hour early and was walking past Elysium, when I saw the woman in charge of the guest list opening the doors. I walked up to her and told her I had a hot date and wanted to bring him to Elysium. Could she help me get in? She scanned me

and then said, 'Sure, no problem. What's your name?' We introduced ourselves and I headed off to my date. She hadn't written my name down, so I wasn't sure she would remember me and keep her promise. After dinner, I suggested to my date that we hit a club. He agreed but said he doubted we would get in to any, as it is almost impossible to get into a good club in Central London on a Friday night. As we were approaching Elysium, my newfound ally saw me, said 'Hi Ozana' and asked the bouncer to let me and my date in. And you were wondering how a club could contribute to the success of its guests…

TAKE ACTION NOW!

Write down 5 ideas you will implement to help your customers be more successful and / or to improve their lives:

1. ______________________________

____

____

2. ______________________________

____

____

3. ______________________________

____

____

4. ______________________________

____

____

5. ______________________________

____

____

Tactic #78

Create Clear Accountability within Your Company

Clear Accountability is a matter of well-defined ownership, sound delegation and good coordination within your team.

Accountability is the guiding principle that defines how we make commitments to one another; how we measure and report our progress; how we interact when things go wrong; and whether we take ownership to get things done. It is, in essence, the nerve center of every organization and affects every working relationship and every member of every team.

If this sounds complicated, here is a simple way to understand it. In college I came up with this brilliant idea to grind up chalk and sprinkle it on the professor's seat just before the physics class. No one in the class liked her and we all started imagining how funny it would be to see her skirt covered in chalk. Of course no one wanted to do it. As I had come up with the idea, I felt somehow Accountable, so I followed through. I accomplished something I was Accountable for (and yes, I was the one who was punished!)

You need to get your employees to be Accountable and do the things they need to do. In some companies one person performs more roles, but in other companies people work across various departments. Everyone wants things done quickly, which is impossible in many circumstances. People report to different managers for various tasks or responsibilities. So the more Accountable your staff are, the more structured the work will be and the more tasks will be accomplished.

If Accountability does not exist in your organization, then every effort toward performance improvement will be inefficient and ineffective. The ability to execute and deliver results is directly tied to the Accountability attitudes, practices and Systems that are in place in your company.

However, the real value and benefit of Accountability stems from the ability to influence events and outcomes before they happen. The customary view of Accountability fails to recognize that people can gain more from a proactive posture than from a reactive one. **Accountability will increase the responsiveness of your company to the Needs of your customers.**

How to ensure Accountability (and how not to)

A real estate agency has to send weekly emails with new property alerts. Imagine the director of the agency says to his team: 'Please gather the offers we receive each week, and send these out to our database weekly.'

Now imagine he says this: 'Person A will collect all sale and rental offers and upload the information to our website within 24 hours of receipt of the offer. Person B is responsible for email marketing and will send the email highlighting new properties every Wednesday at 4 pm. This means person B will have to prepare the newsletter by noon on Wednesday and get my approval between 12 pm and 3.30 pm. If I am not available to review it, person C will do so. If person C is not available, person B will send the email without any third-party review.'

In the first scenario 'the team' was responsible for sending emails, which left completing the task at their discretion. 'The team' means no one is actually being held Accountable. In the second scenario, however, responsibilities for sending the email alerts are clearly split between the team members and each member has clear and specific tasks and deadlines; i.e. they all know what they need to do and by when.

Some of the root causes for lack of Accountability include miscommunication from leaders and misunderstanding from employees. In other words, you say one thing and your employees understand another. This usually happens because you either do not have everything clear in your head, or are not able to express yourself so that people can understand you. The first step in creating Accountability is therefore to find out which it is, and make sure you communicate clearly with your staff, so they are able to be Accountable.

TAKE ACTION NOW!

Write down 5 ideas you will implement in the next 30 days to increase Accountability within your team:

1. ____
____
____

2. ____
____
____

3. ____
____
____

4. ____
____
____

5. ____
____
____

Tactic #79

Understand Your Business. Really!

Look beyond your direct competition to understand what business you are really in.

How can I ask you, the owner of your business, to understand your business? Well, most business owners I meet don't understand. (Of course, you may be the exception.) Ask yourself: 'What business am I really in?' If you sell clothes, you may say you are in fashion. But if you are selling high-end clothes that are associated with a certain status, you may in fact be in the 'status' business (like Rolex).

When you consider your industry, think of why your customers buy from you. What Need do your customers satisfy with your product? What are the uses of your product? ***Chunk Down*** and ***Chunk Up*** to look at your business from different perspectives (see Tactic #36 'Be Efficient with Your Time' for more on Chunking). Let's assume you sell diesel cars. If you Chunk Down, you look at the type of car you offer: a five-seater five-door vehicle that uses diesel. However, if you Chunk Up, you are in the transportation business – you help people move from one point to another and you offer mobility. When you Chunk Down you look at your Competition strictly as other diesel cars. But if you Chunk Up, your Competition could easily be car rental companies, train companies, bus companies, the metro – anything that offers people mobility.

Once you know what business you are really in, it is time to understand what you are good and bad at. Have you been pitching yourself in the wrong industry? Be clear on why you have achieved your current level of success, and examine why you have not achieved more success.

See it in action!

Think of Godiva, the expensive Belgian chocolate. Are they in the chocolate business? You may say, 'Of course!' but I would argue they are in the gifts business. How many times have you bought Godiva chocolates for yourself to eat? How many times have you bought Godiva to offer as gifts? I'm guessing more often for the latter.

So, the same product (chocolate) with different packaging and positioning competes with different types of products or brands (luxury items or gifts).

When you have it clear in your mind what your True Industry is, your entire marketing Strategy becomes focused on what you really are. You don't want to focus on other chocolate makers as your Competitors, and just have different packaging and position. Godiva uses the superior quality of their chocolate and attractive packaging to compete in the luxury goods industry. Thus, Godiva can command higher prices.

TAKE ACTION NOW!

Write down what type of business you are in.

____

Write down 5 elements you could improve on now that you know your True Industry.

1. ____

2. ____

3. ____

4. ____

5. ____

Tactic #80

Clarify Your Vision

Your challenge as a business owner should not be to keep your business on track but rather to make sure you are on the right track and switch to a better one if you are not.

Now that you really understand your business and which industry you are competing in, you need to decide where you want to go. Note that I didn't say where you are going – I said where you want to go. Do you want to be in this industry? Is this the right time to be in this industry? Are you passionate about this industry? Will it be thriving 10 years from now, or will it collapse and be replaced by something else? If the latter, what might that new future look like?

Traditionally, my company raised funds for small- and medium-sized companies. When Romania joined the EU in 2007, however, I started adding grants to my fundraising portfolio. With the banks disinterested in financing anything during the economic crisis, I ended up doing only EU funding of grants. There were fun times, and we managed to be among the top 10 consulting firms specialized in EU funding in Romania. However, a few years down the line I asked myself the questions above and realized I no longer wanted to be in this industry. In the EU funding industry, you are extremely busy during the submission process – the team does not sleep for days as deadlines approach – and this alternates with very quiet periods when there are no calls for proposals or projects open. We were also totally dependent on the Romanian authorities to evaluate the projects we submitted, and at times it could take three years to get your result! In that time the company might manage to complete the project for which it required funding, or it might abandon the project entirely due to market changes.

My Goal had been to help more clients get EU funding grants. After realizing this was not the right industry to be in, my Focus changed towards helping small businesses grow significantly.

Give it some thought!

List today's most successful companies with the fastest growth rates. Google, Apple, Facebook, Groupon, eBay, Amazon, PayPal, Booking.com… did you know these companies 15 years ago? Could you have imagined the types of services they offer 15 years ago? Do they influence the way we do business today?

How will your industry be shaped by such companies? Internet and Technology are changing the business environment extremely quickly, and you need to be among the few winners, not the many losers. You certainly don't want to have been in printed media or a travel agency in the traditional sense. Now rethink your industry, your position, and try to anticipate the future. If you struggle to see those opportunities, use the tools on my website (www.tooliers.com) to diagnose your business's Growth Potential and Challenges. You will immediately see what you are missing.

When you create your Vision, you need to ensure your business model is: sustainable, predictable, consistent. Clarify the Vision for yourself and for your team. Make sure you write down where you want to get and have a good plan on how to get there. Share this with your team. (See Tactic #51 'Share Short-Term and Medium-Term Goals with Everyone in the Company' for more tips of setting and communicating your Goals and Vision.)

TAKE ACTION NOW!

Write down 5 ideas on your Vision for your business (and try to anticipate the future):

1. ______________________________

2. ______________________________

3. ______________________________

4. ______________________________

5. ______________________________

Tactic #81

Create an Unstoppable Pre-emptive Anti-competition Strategy

Use Pre-emptive Strategies to be one step ahead of your Competitors.

A ***Pre-emptive Anti-competition Strategy*** is a strategy designed to prevent any effective Marketing- and Sales-related actions from the Competition, and to encourage ***prospects*** to buy from you. It's a mouthful, I know, so let's go with an easy example: in your college years, you liked a girl. The problem was that many others guys liked that girl too; you had Competition. So you invite her to go to the prom with you. If she says yes, you have stopped your Competitors from being with her. There is only one prom! You win!

In business, Pre-emptive Strategies offer the best opportunity to gain advantage over your Competitors. **Pre-emptive Strategies involve moving first to secure an advantageous position that rivals are foreclosed or discouraged from duplicating, or find impossible to do.** If you master this, you will attract buyers over all of your Competitors. And if you don't do it, your Competitors will.

Think of the girl in the above example as the only Resource available to produce product X. How would your company do if you were the one securing this Resource? You would be the only one able to produce product X of course. As a result you obtain a monopoly position for product X. This outcome may sound too good to be true… and it is. There are always more Resources available, and other types of products or Substitutes. Nonetheless, here are some examples of viable strategies you could consider to pre-empt your Competition:

- Secure exclusive or dominant access to the best distributors in an area.
- Secure the best geographic locations. If you sell flowers, you want to be in a busy intersection or metro station or railway station, where you have loads of traffic. If you want to significantly expand your business and pre-empt your Competitors, you need to open a flower shop in all such busy locations in your town.
- Tie up the best (or the most) raw material sources and / or the most reliable, high-quality suppliers via long-term contracts or backward

vertical integration (when you produce your own raw materials) This move can relegate rivals to struggling for second-best supply positions.

- Last but not least, use ***Educational Marketing*** to 'educate' your market to use the 'right' ***Buying Criteria***, which of course lead to your product being the natural choice, the only choice they consider.

Learn from the best!

You feel like a soda so you head to a corner shop, where Coca-Cola and a no-name cola are available. Which do you choose? Most people choose Coca-Cola; they might not even see the no-name cola. Why? Because Coca-Cola pre-empted their Competition by building a formidable brand.

TAKE ACTION NOW!

Write down 5 ideas to implement and create a Pre-emptive Anti-competition Strategy:

1. ______________________________

____

____

2. ______________________________

____

____

3. ______________________________

____

____

4. ______________________________

____

____

5. ______________________________

____

____

Tactic #82

Inspire High Levels of Brand Loyalty

Think big: Branding is not for big businesses only.

Before we talk about Brand Loyalty, let's get clear on what a *brand* is.

In December 2013, my partner and I went to the Rainmakers Summit, a Business Growth Workshop, in Las Vegas on a two-for-one ticket. He wasn't particularly keen to attend the summit (I was the one who wanted to go) and, while preparing for the trip, he said to me: 'If I don't like it, I will spend the day by the pool.' He was expecting temperatures of 86° Fahrenheit. We live in Europe and the only exposure he'd had to Las Vegas was through movies. All those wild and fun movies took place in a hot and sunny climate – based on what he knew and had seen, he associated Las Vegas with great weather. This is branding! I'm not sure anyone set out to create such a brand for Las Vegas, but in my partner's mind, Vegas meant sun and loads of fun. Needless to say, it was below zero in Vegas during our visit, and when we went for a breath of fresh air at the Voodoo Club, on the roof of Rio All Suits Hotel, we felt as if we were on top of a mountain, ready to go skiing.

Your company's Brand is what people say about your company when you are not in the room, when you can't influence them.

As for Brand Loyalty, it is the degree to which a consumer consistently purchases the same brand within a product class. This means that when you go to the supermarket to purchase your washing liquid or toothbrush, you get the same brand each time, often without even thinking about it. Now it is time to think: why do you always purchase that brand? Because you know it delivers results. You trust this brand. You are so loyal that you don't even realize there are other brands out there that are equally good, or perhaps better!

You might argue, 'But I am not Colgate or Coca-Cola. Why would I create such a powerful brand?' True, but you can be the Colgate or the Coca-Cola for your target market, for your Best Customer. **You want your Best Customer to buy your product without questioning why, and without wondering what the alternatives are.**

Get it right!

A client said to me: 'I sell garbage bags via supermarkets. I don't interact with the end-user.' He defined his client as the supermarket's merchandise buyer, not the customer at the till. 'Plus, everybody wants to buy the cheapest bag,' he continued.

It is true that everyone wants to buy the cheapest bag – provided they are all equal. But they are not. Some bags are thinner and they break while you take your garbage out if you overfill them. If you haven't experienced this it's because the seller of garbage bags in your area does a good job in educating you how to choose your bags or you've learnt through trial and error. And you get the right bag. That is the Best Value for money. When I explained to my client that he needs to stay close to his end-user and that he needed to educate him, and build Brand Loyalty, the penny dropped. His face lit up and he said: 'You are so right! Why did I never think about this? My bags are the best option, and they should be the most expensive, and people should buy them.' He then immediately brainstormed ways to create videos on YouTube showing his bags compared to others, to make in-store promotions, and to be close to his customers. Once customers understand the difference, they of course prefer his bags. And this is how they become loyal to his brand – which, when I initially spoke to him, did not even exist!

Once he had achieved Brand Loyalty, his customers not only committed to his bags, they also told their friends his bags are the best choice. Word of mouth is the cheapest and most effective marketing tool. And yes, you can achieve it with Brand Loyalty.

Have a think: when you last bought a product you loved, did you associate it with the brand? Did you then buy other products from the same brand? Did you tell your friends how happy you were with that product? This is Brand Loyalty.

If you are used to buying Hugo Boss suits, when the crisis comes and you make less money, what do you do? Do you buy Zara suits or do you wait until you can afford another Boss suit? Did you know that these brands are the least affected by adverse economic situations? The reason? People get *emotionally* attached to their favorite brands and they stick to them no matter what.

Now start developing your own brand, no matter what you sell! If you are a

very small business, your Personal Brand will be the brand of the business. So go build your Personal Brand. (See Tactic #59 'Brand Yourself' for some additional tips.)

Brand Loyalty equates to Long-term, Sustainable Business Success. You can count on loyal customers to keep buying your branded products and telling their friends about them. There is a value to that loyalty that correlates directly to brand equity, and therefore with the value of your whole company, which is directly linked to your future performance.

TAKE ACTION NOW!

Write down 5 ideas you will implement in the next 30 days to strengthen your or your company's Brand and increase Brand Loyalty:

1. ______________________________

2. ______________________________

3. ______________________________

4. ______________________________

5. ______________________________

Tactic #83

Build Trust, Credibility and Respect

Trust, Credibility and Respect are the key ingredients to acquiring both engaged employees and loyal customers.

Trust is the firm belief or confidence that a person or thing can be relied upon. If you buy a DVD player you expect it to work. You trust the seller / producer to give you a good, working DVD player. If you didn't trust the seller / producer, you would not buy the DVD player. No one wants to waste their time or money on a non-functioning product or service.

This is why you have to build Trust, Credibility and Respect for your ***brand***, your business, your products and services – and for everything else you do. This pertains to your Relationships with the outside world (customers, business partners), and with the inside environment (your employees).

'If I don't trust you, I will not view you as credible nor will I respect you. If I don't respect you, I will not see you as credible or trustworthy. If I don't find you credible, I will not trust or respect you.'
(Dale Carnegie)

If your (potential) customers don't trust you, they will simply not buy from you. Your employees will take a similar position. How many people are willing to take or stay in a job in which they have to wonder at the end of the month: will I be getting my pay check or not?

The more trusted you are, the more benefits you will have. Your employees will have greater job satisfaction; they will be more committed and engaged in their work and in their relationship with your company. This leads to improved productivity, greater employee retention and, of course, better customer service, and satisfied and loyal customers.

They walk the talk!

Stanford University consistently produces excellent results. Their graduates achieve on average the highest salary after graduation (any business school ranking will show you this); they find jobs in the shortest period of time; and they can more or less choose whom they work for. Stanford is consistently in the top ten universities worldwide. This is a university you trust to give you a good education and the tools to be successful. Stanford University has built Trust, Credibility and Respect by consistently delivering. So, if you wanted to study an MBA, which university would you want to attend if money or qualifications were not an issue?

Trust, Credibility and Respect are the three main ingredients to creating long-lasting customer engagement. You need all three to be successful because this is the only way to ethically influence the behavior of your ***potentials*** and keep them for the long term. This is about 'earning your influence'. **When you are reliable, deliver at all times and create Value for your customers, you earn the right – and privilege – to influence others. Because they have seen consistent behaviors, actions and qualities and have come to value these, they let down their guard and allow themselves to be influenced by you.**

TAKE ACTION NOW!

Write down 5 ideas to build Trust, Credibility and Respect within and for your company:

1. ______________________________
____
____

2. ______________________________
____
____

3. ______________________________
____
____

4. ______________________________
____
____

5. ______________________________
____
____

Tactic #84

Focus on What People Buy, Not on Your Profits or Sales

Shift the Focus from the sale in sight to Long-term Success by prioritizing your prospective customer's Needs.

There is a reason why you don't achieve the Sales numbers you want, and it is not due to weather or holidays or a bad economy. It is because you don't give your customer what she wants.

Have you ever been to Venice? Piazza San Marco is full of pigeons. Tourists feed them corn, bread and seeds (what the pigeons want) and in return the tourists get to sit among the pigeons and pose for great photos (what they want).

Would you like to have customers flocking to buy your product from you? If you want that, you have to give your customers what they want.

Then apply this to your business: focus on what your customer wants (the pigeons obviously want to be fed!), and you will get the Sales and Profits you aim for. Develop Long-term Sustainability for your business by focusing on your customer's Needs rather than on your own. **Putting the Needs of your customers ahead of your own is the solution for building a thriving business. An intense Focus on results can distract everyone from the Sales process.**

Customers don't care about your need to sell. They are concerned only with solving their problems. So focusing your Strategy to demonstrate how your Solution provides the greatest Value in solving their problems is key to your success.

This is what we like to see!

I am often criticized for not 'selling'. Well, I don't like selling, because I don't like to be sold to. When I meet ***prospects****, I genuinely try to solve their problem and provide valuable information. I come up with Solutions and suggestions and I treat their business as if it were mine, providing the best advice I can. Last year, I was driving back to Bucharest from a meeting in Iasi, and I stopped in Roman to have dinner with the owner of a hotel there. She had fully refurbished the hotel to high international standards, but she had no customers. I gave her loads of suggestions during dinner. Instead of a relaxed dinner, it transformed into a work session. She wrote down lots of actions to take. She was very keen, open and took plenty of notes. I liked it that she was so actively involved, so I offered to stay overnight and spend the following morning with her, working on her marketing plan. So we did.*

The morning session was even more packed with actions and ideas. By noon, she had written about 15 pages in her notebook. And then she said: 'Ozana, you seem so knowledgeable about the subject… why don't you do it for me?' I landed a long-term contract for my consulting company, without me even thinking about selling it. Within one month we increased her Sales by 30% and we got a decent income out of this. I focused on her Need – to help her get customers – and my results (which I hadn't expected) came soon afterwards.

TAKE ACTION NOW!

Write down 5 Needs for which your product / offering is providing:

1. __________

2. __________

3. __________

4. __________

5. __________

Tactic #85

Associate with Trusted Organizations

As a new brand you can borrow popularity from Established Organizations.

Association is a smart and fast way to gain authority and credibility for your own business. Being associated has many advantages, from having access to your partner's business customers (see Tactic #13 'Market to Your Partners' Customers') to borrowing influence from them. If your business is small at first, you can try to Affiliate with a better and well-known business to help solidify your business foundation. **If you are Affiliated with a well-known business, your own business itself will grow and increase in trust and influence.** That is why Affiliation is important early on in order to grow your business faster and more easily.

Have you ever broken down in the middle of the street and needed help to push your car to the side? You created an 'Association' with the aim of moving your car out of the way. What alternatives did you have? To call AAA and get them to move the car – but that would have taken longer. And what if you didn't have AAA membership? The Association you created was free, quick and easy and, most importantly, it solved your problem instantly.

What if you could apply the same technique to your business? Here are some examples of Associations you could create, and why:

- Affiliation to an international organization. As a hotel owner, you could be Affiliated to the Best Western chain. As a gas station owner you could be Affiliated to Shell. This type of Association adds credibility to your business, which means more Sales in the long term.
- Associate your unknown product with a well-established company. As a new smoothies drinks company, have your product available in all the cafés belonging to a reputable chain. If this is too long a shot, start by having your product sold in a popular local café. This will push the Sales of your product, because that café's customers trust it, and thus trust is 'transferred' to any product in the café.
- Associate with More Successful People. This is called Branding via Association. So you 'borrow' from the brand of the other person for your own advantage.
- Join a Mastermind group. Find the right group for you, one where you can

equally contribute and get good advice. Mastermind groups or communities are meant to help each other do better. The idea of masterminds is that one person can benefit from many other minds giving advice and suggestions to overcome Challenges. You will have access to thought leaders and mentors who can provide you with key business intelligence, helping you manage your business more effectively to achieve better top and bottom line results. For example, I have created the Mastermind Small Business Growth & Success community on Google+ to help small business owners solve their problems and grow their businesses further. https://plus.google.com/u/0/communities/115826724415825833366.

- If these sound too complicated, start by joining a Chamber of Commerce or a Trade Association in your field. This will open doors to the Association's members, so you can explore common interests and potential business opportunities. You will also have more power in your sector, and can influence at a higher level.
- For more ideas on different types of Partnerships, see Tactic #25 'Develop Partnerships'.

This is what we like to see!

As an EU funding consulting firm, we could not voice our problems about the EU funding system in Romania, which was more dysfunctional than functional. Two smart consultants formed an Association, which we joined, along with 50 other EU funding consulting firms. All of a sudden, our voice was being heard by the government officials, and we could contribute to the improvement of the EU funding system.

Developing Long-term Relationships with trusted and reputable partners is essential for Long-term Sustainability of your business. No one person or business can do it all by itself. According to American Business Magazine, 'approximately 85% of all business failures occur in firms that are not members of their trade association'.

TAKE ACTION NOW!

Write down a potential Partnership or Association you will pursue within:
1. International organizations:

____

____

2. Mastermind groups:

____

____

3. Trade associations:

____

____

Tactic #86

Be 'Online Social'

To be or not to be on Facebook? Your future customers are already there and they expect you to join the party.

These days you cannot afford not to be in social media. You have to go where your clients are. Like it or not, they are on Facebook!

Make social media part of your Marketing Strategy; combine it with other marketing tactics. See social media, another communication channel, but one that works two ways: from you to your customers, and from your customers to you.

Make sure you use it to communicate with your clients only once or twice a day, quickly and efficiently. Once you have posted, responded to comments and finished what's required of you, get out of there. Don't get into the trap of wasting valuable time on Facebook! You have work to do!

Turn Facebook on. Turn Facebook off.

If you're a skeptic, you won't expect much out of social media, at least not in the short term. But your clients expect you to be there – and if you don't regularly talk to them in social media forums, your Competitors will.

A great approach to social media is to think of it as a way to engage more with your customers. Use games, special deals, and promotions to keep them close. You might say, 'No, I sell to serious people. They're not on Facebook.' Go search their names and let's talk afterwards. Unless you sell to my father's generation (70+), your clients are on social media.

I confess I was against social media for a long time. I considered it a waste of time. I don't want to know when my neighbor walks his dog, or when my former primary school friend has a new date. But I was convinced by the younger staff in the firm to use it, and I am already seeing the benefits. We share our blog posts, tips and tricks and other info with our audience on social media.

One of the great advantages of social media is the ability to engage with your customers. Communicating with customers who 'like' or follow your page is easy and direct. You are also able to involve your customers more by asking them questions and getting direct Feedback on your product or service. Managing this Relationship can be intensive if you are a big brand (most companies hire Social Media Experts for this purpose), but a key benefit of engaging with your customers is to strengthen Brand Loyalty – customers feel they 'know' you and your brand becomes personal.

Social media also offers some valuable analysis tools for business owners. You can see how many people have viewed your posts, for example, and determine which are more effective in creating Sales and why.

There's more to it than you think!

Summertime Publishing, who helped with the editing of this book, also runs expatbookshop.com, an online portal for books by expats about expat life. Traffic to the website was ticking along slowly until the publishing house created a Facebook page for Expat Bookshop. Suddenly the views per post increased dramatically. One reason is that the Network had increased significantly, as all Summertime Publishing staff had announced the Facebook page to their Networks, who had announced it to their Networks, and so on. As more people 'like' or follow the page, it gains greater publicity and reach. The Facebook page has driven more traffic to the website and those who enjoy the content and find it relevant often subscribe to the blog.

TAKE ACTION NOW!

Write down 5 actions you will undertake in the next 30 days to increase your social media reach:

1. ____

____

____

2. ____

____

____

3. ____

____

____

4. ____

____

____

5. ____

____

____

Chapter 8
Take that Giant Leap

Tactic #87

Embrace Innovation

'Insanity is doing the same thing over and over again and expecting different results.' (Albert Einstein)

Innovation is about doing something new or in a new way. You see Innovation all around you. Let's compare the lives of our great-grandparents with our lives today. How many new things do we have, and how many things are being done differently? If we want to visit a friend, we drive. If the friend lives far away, we catch a flight. If we have a question, we ask Google. If we want to buy a painting from Bali, we transfer the money online and the painting is shipped directly to our house. These are just examples of basic conveniences we have these days.

But what are all these conveniences other than New Solutions to old problems? The Need to see a friend, the Need to get answers, the Need to decorate your house… now think about the Solutions YOU provide. Think about the problems you solve for your customers. Is there any other way to solve the same problem? When you come up with another Solution, you are innovating. You either invent a new product, or you deliver an existing product in a different way. This is Innovation.

When I say embrace Innovation, I don't mean you necessarily have to invent something completely new. (Of course, if you can, that would be great.) The minimum you can do (and should do) is to use Innovation within your existing business. Be aware of New Solutions, and implement them quickly. Various adjustments to what you do may also lead to that big leap into greater success.

Make it work for you!

You run a restaurant. You think: 'People will always eat out, so I don't care about Innovation. I just need an oven, plates and cutlery.' I challenge you to consider that people's tastes change – so you need to revisit your menu. Thanks to Technology, the way restaurants communicate with their customers and market is changing too, so you need to consider new ways of reaching your customers. I have seen restaurants where guests place the order electronically and the waiter's only role is to bring the food to the table. This is 'cool' for the guests and more efficient for the restaurant. Many restaurants use various applications and devices to take the order, monitor inventory and even store information about recipes. Such restaurants haven't

created anything new per se, but they are using the latest discoveries to increase their efficiency. They are innovating. This allows them to give more Value to the customer or greater profits to the owner, both of which are equally important for Long-term Success.

Do you want to take that leap? Do you want to massively grow your business? Because either you get lucky or you innovate. **If you want better results, you need to do something better – or differently. If you want massive increase, you need to make high-impact changes (and remember: sometimes a small change can have greater impact than a big one.)**

Think about it: if you take the same road to get to work every day, you see pretty much the same things every day. Change your route and you will have a different perspective. You may see a new restaurant and decide to take your family there for Sunday brunch, or you may see a cool shop, or simply a tree or a house that you like and that inspires you to make an improvement to your own house.

In your business, use Innovation to achieve better results. In order to innovate, you need to be open to exploring New Ideas, be ready to collaborate and develop the ability to commercialize New Ideas quickly. Embed a 'yes' attitude and mindset. Seize the opportunity to try new things without fear of failure. Every interaction you have with your team and with your customers is an experiment. Every idea is an opportunity to collaborate on creating something unique.

It took Innovation and being open to New Ideas to get my business to where it is today – a quite different and more successful organization to the one I started. When I realized I was in the wrong industry and needed to add other services to my company, I put together a collection of Business Best Practices used by the most successful companies in the world, and used these on our clients, to help them grow their businesses. However, I wanted to be able to expand my company without being dependent on the quality or moods of the consultants I employed. This is how I came up with the idea of building an automatic tool using those Best Practices and identifying the growth potential for our clients and their companies.

Once I had it clear in my mind that the tool would work automatically, I asked myself how I could use this tool to greater impact, to help more small businesses grow. This is how ***Business Lens™*** become available online; it is for any business owner who wants to grow his company. So, based on my Need (or desire) to grow my consulting practice, I ended up creating a tool to be used online by lots of other business owners to grow their companies.

This concept revolutionizes the entire consulting industry; it replaces a lot of manpower with Technology. I am now moving from consulting towards an internet startup: Tooliers®.com will be the place where any small business owner will come to get on the right path to growing their company. This is a huge jump!

TAKE ACTION NOW!

Write down 5 ways you could innovate in your business. These could be 5 actions you haven't considered before, or 5 avenues to explore… anything you can think of!

1. ____

____

____

2. ____

____

____

3. ____

____

____

4. ____

____

____

5. ____

____

____

Tactic #88

Learn from Startups

I have not failed. I've just found 10,000 ways that won't work.' (Thomas Edison)

Got an idea? Go for it. No, I'm not saying invest loads of money building something no one may want. Experiment first. Pivot. Do little things and test them with your customers. You are an established business; you have customers. So each time you have an idea simply ask your customers what they think about it. If you don't have enough customers, or your customers are the wrong type for the New Idea, talk to your business partners or suppliers. If needs be, talk to your neighbors, your team, and even your team's family if they are relevant to your new product!

If they like it, develop it into a concept product; i.e. a product on paper. Only try to sell it to your targeted customers. Only build the product after you have paying customers.

Startups operate on a shoestring budget, yet many are successful in building multi-million dollar Sales. What characteristics do they all have? A Passion for what they do, a motivated team and (very) limited Resources. Can you replicate this? Set up an experiment. Put a team together and give them a project (of course, the team members have to be relevant to the project). Get them to run the project independently from anything else going on in your company. Give them a limited budget, a limited set of Resources and an audacious Goal to achieve within a certain timeframe. Be prepared to accept failure! Not all startups succeed.

Have regular meetings with your project team and be the objective critical eye. If they don't convince you, it may not be the right project. Then reconsider it, or ditch it. Go with your gut feeling, if this is what you relied on when you started your current business. Be prepared to change direction if necessary. Most startups end up in a totally different place than what they expected. Flexibility is key.

If you don't want to be so ambitious as to conquer the world with your New Idea, you can make incremental changes to what you are already doing. Treat every change as an experiment. If the results are positive, the experiment is a success and you move to the next step. If the results are not positive, you either go back one step, or you change direction completely.

Move 'from plan A to the plan that works'. (Ash Maurya)

I like the lean startup philosophy quoted above. Innovation is about the new, the unknown, uncertainty. Don't expect things to be predictable and happen as they do in your traditional business. Make changes, adjust until you make it work – as long as you have the market confirmation: that there is a demand for what you are trying to do, and that people are prepared to pay for the Solution you are developing.

Step-by-step changes and experiments will help you get the right product to market, and in the right way.

Learn from my mistake

I wasted money on building a platform with 16 tools for various aspects of the business – only to discover afterwards that no one used any of it. I had to get to the point of failure to start talking to potential customers. These discussions helped me realize that the website was too complex and complicated, and that customers did not want to invest the time to read through and understand it. So I binned that and started with one tool, which I gave for free. I achieved a 14% conversion rate (a great number) in the first weeks of launching the new site, which was extremely simple. So I had the market's validation: people were interested in my Solution.

However, although my Solution was a diagnostic tool that would tell business owners where they needed to focus to grow their businesses, it didn't tell them how to achieve this. Based on Customer Feedback (yep, this time I was smarter and talked to them), I understood that they wanted something more. They wanted the how to grow their business and fix the problems. So I developed the concept of action plan. I put it on the site, and my conversion rate decreased to 1%. This is because the site was too confusing (again). Fortunately I had installed a monitoring tool and could see the user's behavior on the site. Based on their clicks, I understood what they were interested in, and what was unclear. I made some improvements and my conversion went up to 5% – not as good as the first one, but better than 1%. As I was still not getting the results I wanted, I spoke to the potential customers again. Those conversations helped me redesign my offering, until I managed to get it right and get them to buy.

TAKE ACTION NOW!

Think of an area that's not performing as well as you hoped it would. Write down 5 experiments you will undertake to attempt to improve it:

1. ______________________________

____

____

2. ______________________________

____

____

3. ______________________________

____

____

4. ______________________________

____

____

5. ______________________________

____

____

Tactic #89

Create a Startup Environment

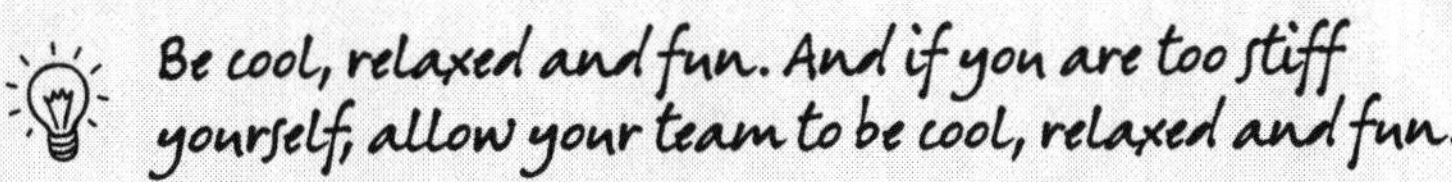

Startups are amazing at achieving great results with small teams and limited Resources. The main ingredient for their success is the Culture and environment that the founders create. Why would you not replicate that in your organization? If not for the entire company, then at least for the team that works on the Innovation project? This is exactly what Steve Jobs did. Apple's epic success, the Macintosh, started as a small side project that had insignificant Resources compared to Apple's mainstream project at the time, the Lisa computer.

Ten ways to imitate a startup

1. **Promote a creative environment.** Encourage your employees to be innovative and implement their personal ideas. By creative environment I mean 'openness', but also the right working space. You may create a separate office for the Innovation team, or you may like to send them for an offsite meeting somewhere unusual to stimulate their creativity and remove them from their daily routine.
2. **Make work schedules flexible.** Startups don't have fixed schedules. You cannot say to your team: now is the time to be creative. Some people are more creative during the night, others get their best ideas while running in the park. Give your Innovation team the freedom to create. No schedule! Of course, you want to know you are paying them for doing the work, so you do need to require some structure and Accountability.
3. **Have transparent communication.** Encourage your staff to share their ideas, bad or good. This sharing has to come from the top. You need to be the first to share. Improve communication within your company by creating transparency and ensuring your employees feel comfortable speaking with top management.
4. **Praise your employees for their accomplishments.** Startups don't have money to pay bonuses, but they nonetheless have very committed people. One reason is that the achievements of the team or individual are recognized. Tell employees that they are doing a great job, that you appreciate their work. This Motivation can buy you a lot more commitment than a bonus would.

5. **Allow room for growth.** Gone are the times when people were promoted based on the number of years they had worked in a position. If someone is good, promote her! She deserves it! Plus, she will maintain her Motivation and will be even more dedicated to your company.
6. **Challenge your employees.** Startups provide challenges every day for the team, which then constantly learns and develops. Why not trust your staff and provide them with more challenges? Help them grow and they will contribute even more. Keep them on the edge with new challenges.
7. **Encourage continuous learning.** Startups learn constantly – often from their mistakes and failures. You don't need your team to fail to learn though. They can attend courses, or work in various departments to expand their mind, skills and understanding.
8. **Create an appealing work environment.** Startup teams love to work. Be it in their garage, their kitchen or in a park. Create a fantastic environment for your staff. Bring a pool table into the main office, or offer them a massage every Friday. Step out of the comfort zone of the established company and behave differently.
9. **Work hard, play hard.** Take your team out, have fun. Celebrate achievements. Encourage them to let their hair down and party. Stiffness is for the boardroom, not for everyday life.
10. **Ask for input.** Startups value this from their employees. Whether you're making a change to the company or looking for advice on how to improve Sales, ask your employees for ideas. Ask them to provide Feedback during your decision-making process.

TAKE ACTION NOW!

Write down 5 actions you will take in the next 30 days to create a more relaxed working environment at your company.

1. ____
____
____

2. ____
____
____

3. ____
____
____

4. ____
____
____

5. ____
____
____

Tactic #90

Follow Your Passion

Explore further what you like doing, and create products around that.

What are you passionate about? Why did you initially start your business? What is your biggest Passion?

Recently I had a conversation with a man whose business was dying. In fact it was not even a proper business: just a website that was generating a little money, enough for the owner to hang on and hope. He had realized though that he needed to do something else. He kept telling me he didn't know what that might be; that he had tried everything possible. During that conversation, I asked him for Feedback on my website. He was brilliant. He was able to tell me things that no highly paid consultants had spotted. I made a comment about his abilities to criticize websites and he admitted that this is what he loves doing. This is his Passion. Would you not want someone like him to critique your website, so that you could know exactly what to improve and how to provide a better experience for your customer?

He went on to set up a new business doing exactly this: assessing websites. He is now combining his Passion with a big Need in the market, and he is making much more money than what he was making with his previous website. All it took was one conversation!

Perhaps you are not passionate about your product; you just started your business because you saw an opportunity and today you are making money. That's fine. But you must be passionate about something you do in that business. It could be that you like talking to your customers, or that you like choosing your raw materials… whatever it is, identify it, and think how you can do more and better with what you enjoy doing.

Let me tell you my story…

In 2004 I set up a consulting firm as a 'bridge' between UK and Romania. There were a lot of business people in the UK asking me for help with my Romanian connections. They were looking for anything from setting up a new production facility in Romania to buying an existing business to employing IT specialists. Being from Romania and having had my professional training in London gave me the edge to develop a successful business. This business was based on my connections, skills and abilities, and on a niche in the market, where there was clearly a Need. But the economic crisis put all big projects on hold and my business almost went bankrupt… this is when I realized that my Passion was actually to help other businesses make money; that I was most thrilled when a project succeeded, because that us when I saw the Value in what we did for the client. This Passion, combined with a large library of Best Practices that successful businesses use, led to me being very successful with Tooliers®, my online platform with tools to help small businesses grow.

Although I didn't start out with any Passion as such (see above), I discovered my Passion later and aligned my business with it. And it is only then that I achieved success. Before that, I made a decent living, but I couldn't really call it a successful business. The Breakthrough came when I could put my finger on my Passion and use it to serve others.

The three main ingredients for success: be passionate about what you do; provide Value to the customer; have a big enough market for your offering.

TAKE ACTION NOW!

Identify your Passion(s):

____

____

____

Write down 5 ideas to connect your Passion to your business, or to connect your business to your Passion:

1. ____

2. ____

3. ____

4. ____

5. ____

Tactic #91

Bring New Voices into Your Company

By New Voices I mean new people from outside of the company who generate different thinking, different perspectives, and different views. Anyone can be a New Voice. Really! It could be the teller when you do your weekly groceries shopping, or a highly regarded businessperson. You may be surprised to find that your child can generate a New Perspective for you, or can trigger an idea for a new product. Of course the quality of the New Voice influences the quality of the information you receive.

Even people you think are less qualified to give you advice can help. You never know where the great idea will come from. Be open!

The best New Voices are usually consultants, coaches or trainers. But you can also just have a monthly meeting with a few of your friends who run other types of businesses and exchange ideas. Make a habit of sharing what works in each business, and try to apply those techniques in your business. Alternatively, use Tooliers®.com, which shows you the whole picture of your company and what you lack for your further growth. It also gives you step-by-step actions to use and implement the latest business concepts and discoveries into your business, based on your specific Needs (which are uncovered with the diagnosis).

An example of bringing together New Voices is Mastermind Small Business Growth & Success, a free community on Goggle+. The community is all about helping business owners grow their businesses. You can post specific questions and challenges and receive answers from community members. (I personally commit 10 hours per month to answer questions.)

Don't try to do everything by yourself; it is simply impossible. New Voices can bring New Perspectives, make you see things you have not considered before. **You may get an idea that can bring thousands or millions of dollars in additional Sales for your business. Or you may get an idea that can save thousands or millions for your business. Or you may simply save a lot of time for yourself.**

Don't overlook a potential New Voice

I had a student telling me in early 2000 that I had to blog. My reaction was: Who are you? Why would I waste time writing, when I could use my time on something else? What I am doing now? Blogging! Would I have been further ahead of Competitors if I had listened to him at the time? Yes!

Since I've come to understand how important it is to bring New Voices into my business, I am always open to observing, to talking to people. I know a lot about business, but I constantly add to my Knowledge.

Now we're talking!

I've mastered Facebook and LinkedIn for Marketing and Sales, but I still don't get Twitter. Recently I met with an entrepreneur in Belgium who had seen one of my presentations. We had an exploratory discussion, and we both learned from each other: I shared some tricks we use on Facebook (he loved them!) and he shared tips on using Twitter. If, at the time of reading this book, I have a significant number of followers, it worked!

TAKE ACTION NOW!

Write down 5 New Voices you will bring into your business (this could be a consultant or advisor, participating in a Training workshop, chatting to a partner about each other's business Challenges, or checking out Tooliers®.)

1. ____

____

____

2. ____

____

____

3. ____

____

____

4. ____

____

____

5. ____

____

____

Tactic #92

Bring in Experts

You know your company inside out. You may even know your industry inside out. But you can't know everything about business in general. These days, everything is changing so fast, that is impossible for one person to keep up with everything. Everything is highly specialized these days. If you want to master everything, you can't apply anything. You will spend so much time on learning that you won't have time to implement.

You can't be the Expert in everything in your business. You can become an Expert, but is it worth the time you spend learning about the subject?

You have an accountant, right? Do you follow how tax rules and other legislation change, or do you rely on your accountant to tell you and to implement them in your business? Surely the latter (unless this is a real interest of yours)! Why not rely on other Experts in very specialized fields to broaden your horizon and help you take your business to the next level?

Here's why you need to do this!

Consider the case of a famous architect who needs a new website. He doesn't know how to build websites and his team members don't know either. His best Solution is to outsource this task to an Expert. The Expert may charge the architect more than what he earns (if he considers the hourly rate), but could he do this work himself? If he were to learn website development, he would spend a lot more time on the project, and it would end up even more expensive. He needs to accept paying for (what appears to be expensive) outside help to get the job done, while he focuses on what he is good at: designing houses.

From my professional experience, I find that the strengths of a company tend to align with the owner's Skills and Passions. If the owner is good at creating products, the company will have a great product. But the same owner can't necessarily sell – so the company may find it barely sells its great products. The owner that is great at selling may be a disaster when it comes to organizing – and so his company will be weak in this area. No individual knows it all or can do it all, or is good at it all. Companies are the same. There are only a few companies in the world that are good at everything – and you know them. Brands like Google, Apple, Amazon, Coca-Cola are great at everything.

If you want to be good at everything and become big and famous you need to first understand what you are not good at and address those areas (remember Tactic #37 'Strengthen the Weakest Link'?). Either develop Expertise in-house, or bring it in from outside. Give the jobs you are bad at to people who are top of that class, and your business will thrive. **I don't agree that we have to work on improving everything we are bad at. For maximum efficiency and best results, bring in people who are passionate about those areas, and let them improve your business.**

I once met a self-made millionaire who subcontracted almost everything. When I asked if he has studied law to draft such great contracts, he said he employs great lawyers. When I asked if he read his own financial results, he said he has a great CFO that does it for him. When I asked him if he skis, he said: 'No, I have others do it for me, so I can enjoy this glass of wine with you.'

Do it right!

What do you know about video marketing? At the time of writing this book, YouTube is the SEO Wild Wild West. With the right technique, anyone on YouTube can bring loads of traffic to their website. Do you know you can also have (almost) free advertising on YouTube? If you put a video up there advertising your service and choose to pay per click, you only pay if someone watches your video for more than 30 seconds. If the person clicks 'skip ad' before 30 seconds – and most people do – you don't pay anything. If someone watches more than 30 seconds, you pay. But you have a qualified Lead and that is something worth paying for.

So now you know what you need to do: shoot a video, upload it to YouTube, create a campaign for it, and watch the traffic coming to your website. Sounds simple right? But it's only simple if you're an Expert and know how to do it. Try do it yourself: by the time you have figured it all out, YouTube may have changed the rules. You either move fast and do it properly – through an Expert – or you miss an opportunity.

Use the best Expert in the field. Pay more than you had expected. It is worth the investment.

TAKE ACTION NOW!

Write down 5 areas in your business for which you could do with external Expertise:

1. ____

2. ____

3. ____

4. ____

5. ____

Tactic #93

Bring the Person(s) You Need into Your Business Today

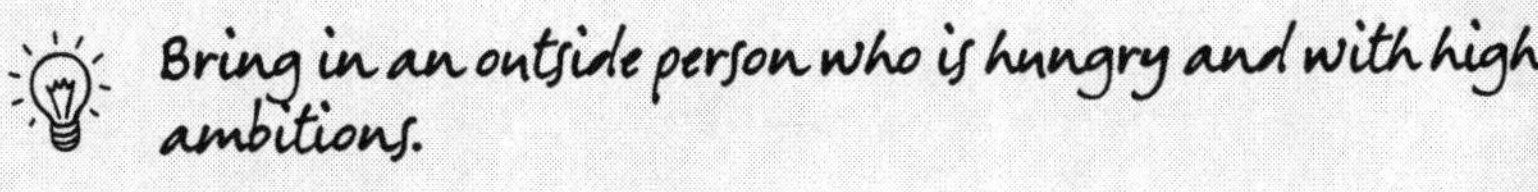

You have built a successful company, but you have reached a plateau. Or your business is growing but not at the double or triple digits you want. You have got New Voices that generated New Ideas and now it is time to implement these. Your options are to use existing Resources or to recruit new people. Which do you go for?

I encourage you to be brave and recruit. You want a big jump, right? Those already in your company are used to a certain way of doing things. They are comfortable where they are and it is not easy to change people. Besides, you recruited them for the existing jobs, or even for old jobs that changed over time. Right now, you need fresh blood in your business.

Bring someone from outside that has the drive you have. Of course you want the Skills, but you also want the commitment and the hard work. You want a can-do, unstoppable attitude. If everyone in your company has this attitude, then great, just promote some of your Resources to get involved with the new projects. But I doubt you have it. And if you do, you are ahead of me, and may not even need this book.

Take time to assess your company in the current economy, in your industry today. Your big plans may or may not be linked to your current activities. You may need New Skills. You may need some specialized expertise. You may need the latest discoveries in various business aspects brought into your business. Unless your people have been continuously Trained and have kept up with new developments in fields that matter to your new projects, you are better off bringing people from outside. **Consider bringing in a combination of employees and short-term Experts. The Experts may cost you more per hour or job, but they do the right thing faster, and to high standards.**

If you can bring in a new partner, go this route. You may be tempted to keep the whole pie for yourself, but it is best to have a smaller part of a bigger pie than to have 100% of a small pie. You want to share responsibilities as well as the glory. You want a partner that may be keener even than you are! Someone fresh! That person brings the execution, implementation, but also more ideas and viewpoints.

This is the partner I have just brought into my business

I have achieved a lot by myself. I have built great knowledge, great tools, and I have helped hundreds of business owners massively grow their companies, but I realize there is a limit to what I can do myself. Up until recently, I have been coordinating the development of Tooliers® (my startup platform with business growth tools); the marketing and execution of our ***Business Doctor*** *(consulting division); and the development of the tools and growth programs. However, since I brought in Catalina, both a former vice-president of a multinational bank and general manager of the largest health company in Romania, things have been moving ahead exponentially. This is because she is now coordinating all the efforts in Romania, which allows me to fully concentrate on the international front. Plus, Catalina has brought in some great ideas, which we are now working on implementing. Just imagine: how would it feel to have* ***another you*** *in your company? That person exists, and it is your job to find her and bring her into your business.*

TAKE ACTION NOW!

Write down 5 characteristics of the New Person you want to bring into your business today:

1. ____

2. ____

3. ____

4. ____

5. ____

Tactic #94

Fire the Person Holding You Back

A Good Employee yesterday may be a Bad Employee tomorrow.

People have always been, and probably will always be, the single most important asset to any organization. At the same time, people can be the biggest problem in any organization.

Keeping an employee who isn't contributing positively can really hurt your company, especially if you have a small business in which Culture is closely tied to success. A Bad Employee can be a rotten apple in your company. Strong negativity, a poor attitude, backbiting, and incompetence can spread quickly within your company. Co-workers typically try to fight off or resist catching the negative traits, but they tend to be contagious and can severely hurt or even kill a company. Besides, the employee is holding the place of someone else who could truly contribute and help the team.

Any one of your employees can become a Bad Employee for multiple reasons: they may be resistant to change, they may not like the new direction, or they may need change, which your company is not providing. They could simply get bored in their job, or acquire other interests or require more challenges... analyze your employees constantly and change them if they are no longer appropriate for your business. Of course, try to identify the cause of the mismatch first and try to fix it. But if this is not possible, break the bond and offer yourself, your team and that person an exit from a poor working environment.

Here's why you need to do this!

I once had a great consultant who managed to find creative Solutions for most of our projects. He brought business in, managed project delivery, and really helped everyone in the company. He had been with us for seven years and he knew everything about our business. He was extremely valuable. However, when I came in with New Ideas, although he liked them, he wasn't keen to be involved. Within months he became resistant. He simply shut himself off from the new direction I wanted the company to take and started finding faults in everything we were doing.

My advisers told me to fire him. But I couldn't. They told me that his lack of Motivation and bad attitude would rub off on other employees. I understood this, and I saw it happening, but I still could not let him go. He had been with us for so long – a lot of our achievements were due to him. How could I let go such a great person? What about our personal connection? Our relationship had gone beyond employee–employer. We went skiing together, we attended parties and other social activities, we even made some investments together.

One year later and I still had no results from this employee. I had to do something – so I gave him targets to accomplish within the new direction, which meant he had to accept the new direction and deliver, or he wouldn't get paid. Unfortunately, he didn't deliver, and thus he didn't get paid. Within a month, he had left. Today he does what he was doing for us in another company. He is happy doing what he wants to do – and we are happy about not having to carry someone who doesn't contribute.

TAKE ACTION NOW!

Identify 3 people within your company that you consider to be Bad Employees or a bad influence. Mention why for each person.

1. ____

____

____

2. ____

____

____

3. ____

____

____

4. ____

____

____

5. ____

____

____

Tactic #95

Know Exactly Where Your Business Is TODAY and Anticipate TOMORROW

Just as you wouldn't sell horses for transportation, as the car has been invented and does a better job, you wouldn't want to set up a large national newspaper today, because everything is moving towards digital media. You may have the best product on the planet, but if the world has moved away from using that type of product, your business will die.

Know exactly where your industry is today.

As a business owner, you must understand what is going on not just in your own business but also in your entire industry. **Reflect regularly on your industry to understand what Stage it is at right now, and where it is heading. Understand the industry challenges of both today and tomorrow.**

Make it work for you!
Travel agencies have suffered since the advent of the internet. People are now booking flights, accommodation and even complete holidays online. There is no need to speak to a travel agent anymore. The information is available online. Unless you are in a niche market, or offer high-end holidays, it is highly likely you will be out of business soon. But what if you anticipated this change five years ago, or even 10 years ago? Maybe you would be Booking.com!

Don't hide from the truth: the factors that affect the entire industry do (or will) have an impact on your business. While you arguably can't control these external factors, you can control how your business will respond to them. Such factors can hurt you – or they can help you, if you know how to use them to your advantage.

Do you like your industry? Can your business produce the results you expect in your industry? These are other questions you need to ask yourself. You may remember that my consulting company used to help organizations in Romania get EU funding (grants for investment projects to help the country develop faster). Despite the potential for huge consulting fees, I realized this is not a good industry to be in. Why? Not because of Competition or New Technologies, but because the system is dysfunctional and the Romanian

authorities incompetent. This is unlikely to change. The result is that nothing is predictable, that a professional service becomes a lottery. You may do a great job, but not get grants for your clients because the people working in the system do not follow clear rules and procedures.

As mentioned earlier, another drawback of this industry is that you alternate between times of high-intensity work and times of almost no work. So you have peaks in which your Resources (staff) are stretched, and then you have lows, when your consultants have nothing to do.

It was clear to me that a consulting business cannot be sustainable in this industry. This is when I came up with the ***Business Doctor*** service: we perform a diagnosis on companies to identify where they are leaving money on the table, make a plan with them to grow their business and help them implement it. With this ***Complementary Service***, we have constant work for our consultants. In EU funding peak times the entire team is busy with preparing projects for grant proposals and in between calls for proposals, our consultants work on Business Doctor.

If I had failed to realize the dynamics of the EU grant proposal industry in Romania, and not come up with a future-oriented Solution, the business today would be a struggle to survive – we would be covering the low months (losses) with the profits from peak months.

Know exactly where your company is in its industry today.

Once you understand the nuts and bolts of your industry, reflect on where your company is within that industry. In most industries there are no heroes, just choices. So rather than trying to be all things to all people, position your company in your niche, and aim to dominate that niche.

Now we're talking!

Our tools on Tooliers® perform miracles on businesses that want to grow, businesses that are suffering or businesses that don't know where they are. The same tools can be used by the small business owner and by managers in larger companies. The tools can even be used by banks, private equity funds, rating agencies and many other organizations. When we initially marketed Tooliers®, we were the Solution for everything and everyone. And we sold nothing! Once we took one niche – small business owners committed to growing their companies and who have minimum time and capital to invest in growth – we had targeted messages. This is how we managed to raise interest in the market and then to sell.

TAKE ACTION NOW!

Write down 5 characteristics of your industry today:

1. ______________________________

2. ______________________________

3. ______________________________

4. ______________________________

5. ______________________________

Write down 5 characteristics you think your industry will have in the future:

1. ______________________________

2. ______________________________

3. ______________________________

4. ______________________________

5. ______________________________

Tactic #96

Ensure that Your Company Spots Your Potential Customers' Needs before They Do

Constantly observe your customers' behavior. Look at what makes them happy and what makes them anxious.

If you want to take that big leap forward, you have to **anticipate what your customers will want in future**. This is one of the secrets to the success of Steve Jobs. If he had gone out and asked people whether they wanted an iPad, the answer would have been 'no'. Clients were not aware of their Need. It is Steve Jobs who anticipated and perhaps even created this Need!

A smart application!

Think back to 10 years ago. You had a phone and a camera. And a computer. The phone's job was to make phone calls; to enable you to speak to people not in your vicinity. The camera's job was to take pictures, so you could have memories of places you had visited and people you had met. The computer's job was a little more complex: you could work on Word documents, you could perform calculus and create graphs in Excel, you could create presentations in PowerPoint, you could access the internet, access emails and more. Today, you have smart phones that perform all these jobs.

Did you imagine 10 years ago that one day your whole 'life' would be in one device? Can you imagine your life now without a smart phone? Your Need changed and those companies that anticipated this change are doing very well.

I recently participated in an exercise at a high profile event, in which I had to use customer interviews to identify the characteristics of the future fridge. A fridge is a fridge, right? You store food inside, to preserve it for longer. But when I performed the customer interviews, I was amazed to discover that the majority of interviewees wanted their fridge to do the following: tell me when supplies have run out, tell me when items are about to expire, prepare the meal for me, serve the meal for me.

What's interesting is that none of the people I interviewed had thought of these functions before. Only when I challenged them to tell me what job(s) they would like the fridge to perform, did they reach these conclusions. I dare say there is clearly a Need or a gap in the market for such a fridge! Their reasons were varied: from saving time to relieving the stress of preparing a meal for the family. The fridge manufacturer now knows to design tomorrow's fridge – and he also knows the key elements of his marketing messages.

What does your 'tomorrow product' look like? The answer to this question comes once you have identified your clients' Future Needs.

TAKE ACTION NOW!

Write down 5 problems your customers are facing right now. (These don't have to be those problems for which you are currently providing Solutions. Think of problems relevant to your industry.)

1. ______________________________

____

____

2. ______________________________

____

____

3. ______________________________

____

____

4. ______________________________

____

____

5. ______________________________

____

____

Tactic #97

Identify Your Clients' REAL Needs

Understand WHY people do what they do, not just what they say they do.

Up until few years ago, if you'd asked a CD retailer why customers come to his shop, he would have said 'to buy the CD of their favorite singer'. Steve Jobs realized that they don't buy CDs – they buy music. And he came up with digital music. He satisfied the same Need (to listen to music) in a different way: digital music. If he had sold pink CDs (provided that he wanted to satisfy the Need of buying CDs), would he have been as successful?

In most cases, people are not aware of their real Need

*When I initially developed **Business Lens™**, the tool to show the business owner the naked truth about his business, I asked my friends and existing clients to test it. When I asked a friend: 'What is your biggest business Challenge?' he replied that he didn't have any Challenges. He is well positioned, he has customers and he makes money. He is okay. He just needs to spend most of his time in his pub, but this is the norm in the hospitality industry. If you are not there, the barman steals, the personnel do not clean properly, the waiters do not serve the guests well, and so on.*

I asked him to do me a favor and go through the questions in my Business lens™ and give me Feedback. He spent three hours with us and, when he saw the report, he could not believe it: he had many more problems than he had realized. And the real problem in his business was himself. All of the negative elements of his work were created by his way of thinking and his attitude towards his staff. He thought people in his industry would come and go, that they didn't deserve any Training, or special attention. On reading our report, he realized that it is possible to recruit the right people, and most importantly to develop the right Culture in his company, in order to accomplish his Goals. Now, he hardly spends time at the pub at all. He enjoys holidays, weekends away, time with his family, and his pub makes more money. In fact, he is in the process of opening a pub in another location.

The point is to identify the customer's real Need, a Need that he was not aware of (mostly because he did not know any other way to do things). Do this by showing the client the real problem in his business. There is a difference between what clients want and what they truly need. Find out their underlying Needs, both present and future. This will help you remain relevant, and will lead to that big jump.

Assess your customer's Needs now. Repeat once a year.

TAKE ACTION NOW!

Write down 5 reasons your customers behave the way they do in relation to the type of product or service you offer:

1. ____________________

____

____

2. ____________________

____

____

3. ____________________

____

____

4. ____________________

____

____

5. ____________________

____

____

Tactic #98

Leverage Your Platform for Maximum Results

By Platform I mean your infrastructure, and more. **Your Platform is everything that your company has today: people, assets, products / services, procedures, credentials, brand, reputation.** Think of what your business has, and how you can extract maximum Value from this.

I once met an investment fund manager at Cargill. I was curious to know how one could manage investment funds while working for an agricultural company. He explained that, because Cargill has ***AAA rating***, they can borrow money very cheaply. So they set up an investment fund to make more money. The model is simple: based on their good borrowing capacity, they borrow money (which costs them very little) and use that money to invest in other assets, which make even more money for them; i.e. they Leverage their credibility and use their 'Platform' to make more money.

You don't have to be a multinational company to apply this concept. You may be a small retailer of electronics. Your margins are small, because you can't afford to buy volumes from the supplier that command low prices. An idea for you is to buy a larger quantity, and sell the difference to another retailer just like you: you make a margin on that, as well as obtain a larger margin for your store. If this is not possible due to lack of funds, then associate with another retailer and make a Joint Purchase – this doesn't require any additional investment on your side, but leads to lower prices due to the volume you buy together. Be creative!

This is what we like to see!

At my company, our projects and applications for EU funding for clients became so good that people working in the ministry (whom we had never met) recommended us as consultants. We had no idea this was happening until we received a call from the largest car manufacturer in Romania requesting a meeting to discuss EU Funding. They had been referred to us by the ministry. This opened our eyes and we started actively encouraging authorities to spread the word about our company. This is an unconventional way to Leverage the good work we do, our credentials, the Platform we have, to bring more customers.

Leverage your Platform for now, but more so for the future.

TAKE ACTION NOW!

Write down 5 current qualities or strengths of your company that make up your Platform:

1. ______
2. ______
3. ______
4. ______
5. ______

Write down 5 ideas to further Leverage the above-mentioned strengths:

1. ______
______
______

2. ______
______
______

3. ______
______
______

4. ______
______
______

5. ______
______
______

Tactic #99

Expand Your Distribution Channels

Find creative ways to sell your product. Repackage and Repurpose your product for further reach.

A ***Distribution Channel*** can refer to how you disseminate your product or service as well as new ways of selling your product. Repackaging or Repositioning your product, for example, might result in further reach.

This is how it's done!

As a car manufacturer, you would have to rely on one or more distributors in a territory. Let's imagine you have one distributor in New York, another in Florida, and so on. Traditionally, you would get another distributor for the same territory, or you would go into a new country, where, again, you would look for local distributors. But how about using the internet as your distributor? Mini Cooper offer a great online application to design your own car. The interested buyer can select which features he wants the car to have, and can see the visual – and associated price – online. The distributor is not able to offer such a service, unless he uses the main website. With this tool on their website, BMW (who owns Mini Cooper) removes a fair amount of power from the distributor, as they generate leads online themselves.

One of our clients imports and distributes consumable goods (plastic cups, tissues, garbage bags, to name but a few). They usually sell to large supermarkets, which constantly put pressure on price. So the client made a very clever move: they packaged some of their products for the hospitality industry and offered these online. They created their own Distribution Channel, for this specific target market. It's the same product, but they added Sales by addressing a new market, in a new way.

As a Trainer, you deliver your 'content' to a number of people that gather in a room. There might be 10, 100, 1000 or more participants. But this approach requires your presence in the room, as well as constant marketing to fill up the audience. How about creating a webinar? You could reach people not within your geographical proximity. If you record your presentations or webinars, you could also sell them as products online. The beauty of this is that you make money while you sleep. That same content can bring 10 or 100 or 1000 times more money if you package it differently and sell it online.

In case you haven't realized, I too am expanding my Distribution Channels – with this book. The library of Best Practices, which is the basis of ***Business Lens™*** (our main tool on Tooliers®) is Repackaged here.

TAKE ACTION NOW!

Write down 5 ideas you can implement to Repackage or Repurpose your product:

1. ____
____
____

2. ____
____
____

3. ____
____
____

4. ____
____
____

5. ____
____
____

Tactic #100

Leverage with Technology

Nowadays, Technology is ubiquitous in business. It permeates every aspect of a business and streamlines everything from production and logistics to scheduling and advertising. Keeping up with the rapid advances and changes in Technology is a must, should your business have any hope of keeping up with the market. Any unused technological aid is a potential revenue stream dried up, either through wasteful management or production or simply through missed avenues of reaching customers.

Technology is not something I grew up with, and I don't grasp it as easily as the new generation. But when I saw its power, I became a fan.

Use Technology to make 10 or 100 times more with little or no effort! Automate your processes.

See it in action!

When we started Tooliers®, we were sending emails using Mailchimp (software that distributes your newsletter and messages via email). We were sending campaigns, and we could see who opened our email, who clicked, who unsubscribed, and so on. They have some clever reports, and I was satisfied with their Solution. I wasn't looking for an alternative Solution. Then a contact insisted I take a look at Infusionsoft, which takes things a step further and allows you to Automate marketing messages; i.e. the customer receives a series of emails when you want them to be sent, but without you having to do anything other than the initial programming (email #1 to be sent out within an hour of customer's first contact, email #2 a day later, email #3 a week later, and so on.) Compare this to a newsletter: you send it now and that's it. If a customer signs up tomorrow, she misses the newsletter I just sent.

The great thing with Automating emails is that you squeeze all opportunities to transform a potential lead into a customer and to push Sales to existing customers. **So now, we are not creating campaigns – we are creating Marketing Automation.** We use campaigns, but once a campaign is created it is used for any new potential that comes into our Sales Funnel. With this Technology, we have Automated leads coming in and clients receive automatic campaigns based on their behavior, as well as Automated calls to action, which of course they can take to buy online. This is making money while you sleep.

Once created, such an asset generates money non-stop, no matter what you do and where you are.

I urge you to seek out the Technologies that can help you, and to apply them. **Why pay people to do what Technology can do?** Why do something manually that can be done automatically? Why leave money on the table by not doing things that Technology can do for you?

TAKE ACTION NOW!

Write down 5 Technology ideas or 5 problems you need to solve with Technology that you will research on Google to help your type of business:

1. ______________________________

____

____

2. ______________________________

____

____

3. ______________________________

____

____

4. ______________________________

____

____

5. ______________________________

____

____

Tactic #101

Constantly Look for New Ideas

New Ideas should be the lifeblood of your business. They help you avoid becoming stale and keep you relevant, by giving you options for branching out and diversifying.

Add Looking for New Ideas into your daily routine. Train your team to include it in their schedule too.

Contemplate New Perspectives designed to improve your business. A New Perspective is another way of seeing things, issues, people; it is that different route to get home, or that New Voice you bring into your company. (See Tactic #91 'Bring New Voices into Your Company'.)

Engage in a New Passion that might have as an end result the improvement of your business. New Passion is doing what the company does, in a new way, as best as it can.

Engage in New Experiments designed to improve your business. New experiments are new actions, questions or tactics that generate New Ideas, that lead to Innovation.

Be open to everything around you.

Ask yourself New Questions (ones that have never been asked before in your company), such as:

- If you were going to create another industry, what would it be? Examples of new industries created by companies include: Microsoft – operating systems, Facebook – social networks, Google – internet search and advertising.
- If you were to start your business today from scratch and maximize your impact, leverage and profitability, what would you do? What would your business look like?
- Think about your current reality and ask yourself 'What if' questions.
- Think about the future and ask yourself 'What if?' questions.

- What ***distribution channels*** are you not using, or via which are Sales not being maximized?
- What Technology are you not using? What process have you not Automated?
- What are the trends in the market? Identify changes in the market as early as they appear, and figure out where the market is going.
- What massively improves the lives of your customers? What would wow our customer?

I spend an hour per day…

… gathering New Ideas. I either read a blog post, watch a short video, or simply open emails from our competitors and people I respect and trust (yes, I have signed up to few email distribution lists), and see what they do. I also go to seminars and conferences, and I meet other like-minded people and exchange view-points, what we have done, what we have learned or tried… and I often get ideas from these efforts that I can implement in my business. I either get ideas for marketing (oh, yes, this is a never-know-it-all subject, as things emerge constantly), or for other products. And most importantly, I speak to our customers, as they are the best source for further developments and improvements.

I challenge you to come up with one killer idea, or many improvements to what you are currently doing. That giant leap can be achieved by bringing to the market a wow product, or by making a series of improvements to your business that have a compound effect.

TAKE ACTION NOW!

Write down 5 directions you will consider for generating New Ideas. (You might read a new book, or you speak to someone in particular, or visit a new street in your neighborhood each day…)

1. ____

____

____

2. ____

____

____

3. ____

____

____

4. ____

____

____

5. ____

____

____

Bonus Chapter
Love Letter

I write about giving more Value than anticipated to your clients, about wowing your customers, about giving something for free. Here, it is my freebie to wow you.

This 'Love Letter' is a letter you write as if it was written by your Best Customer to your company. Fill in the blanks. The point of this letter is to help you really understand your business, and what matters for your business's success. It looks like a testimonial, but it is way more than that. Once this letter sounds right, you know the recipe for your business's success. You have clarity about your own business. You just need to execute correctly.

Below you will find a framework for your Love Letter, as well as the letter I wrote for Tooliers®. This helps me 'name' my persona, the benefits of my product (both logical and emotional), the impact my product has on customers' lives, how to find our customers, what to use to find customers, what I want my customers journey to be, how to ask them to provide recommendations, and more.

This framework is basically your Strategy in a nutshell! And yes, you can use this to get inspiration for what you want your (real) client testimonials to look like.

I challenge you to fill in the blanks for your business. If you want the original, so you don't have to type up the framework, visit www.shortcuttobusinesssuccess.com/love-letter/ and request your copy. You will receive it instantly.

Love Letter Framework

Dear **[Enter Company Name]**,

My name is **[Persona's name]** and I must tell you I love your **[product type]** and I feel compelled to tell you my story.

I am a **[business type / life or lifestyle role]** who **[problem / passion statement]**. Thing is, that **[impact of pain / passion to life]**.

But **[Product Name]** changed my life.

Whenever I **[do specific things with product]** it works exactly as promised. Not only do I **[get specific benefits]** but it makes me feel **[strong emotional reaction]**.

I find I use the product in that way every **[time period: hour / day / week, etc.]**

It's as if you looked me in the eye and said, '**[Persona's name]** I promise you **[value promise]**'.

What I didn't expect, and share with other **[why shares with]** by **[mean of 'sharing']** is that you made me feel **[emotion impact].**

Your product has forever **[how life changed]**.

I first heard of your product while **[activity / place related to title / life role]**. I decided to learn if it was really meant for me, so **[how to get more info]** where you said **[key message promise]** which spoke directly to me. To tell you the truth, at first I was skeptical. But then, when you provided **[activity to induce trust]** I knew you were the right company.

[Influencer] endorsing the product was also key.

Still, I felt **[primary concern / objection].**

Finally, when **[final action]** I was ready to **[sign up / buy / try]**.

I couldn't wait to get going, so as soon as I could, I **[first product setup / interaction]** to get started, and very quickly tried the **[feature to realize promise]** which made me feel hopeful that I made the right decision.

Love Letter Example

Dear Tooliers®,

My name is Elisabeth. I must tell you that I love your Marketing Lens Diagnosis and Growth Program™ and I feel compelled to tell you my story.

I am an accounting firm owner who needs more clients. Thing is, I'm not earning enough. But Marketing Lens™ has changed my life.

Whenever I think of investing in marketing activities, I use the Marketing Lens™ and it works exactly as promised. Not only do I discover free ways to attract clients, but it also makes me feel like I really master marketing as a whole. I find myself working on one action to grow my business every other day, for only 15 minutes per day. I started this just one month ago and I already see 10% more enquiries from potential clients.

It's as if you looked me in the eye and said, 'Elisabeth I promise that you will discover ways of getting more customers by yourself without spending a cent.'

What I didn't expect, and I share this with other accounting firm owners in our regular ACCA meetings, is that you made me feel like a great businessperson, not just an accountant. I truly *feel* I own my business now; I am not just a simple accountant, who has a job in my own company.

Marketing Lens Diagnosis and Growth Program™ has forever changed how I market our accounting services.

I first heard of your product while browsing The American Institute of CPAs online. I decided to learn if it was really meant for me and I went to www.tooliers.com. You said that I would get answers to questions I had never asked myself and this really resonated with me. To tell you the truth, at first I was skeptical about getting actions tailored to my business and given automatically to me by a computer! No one knows my industry better than me. But then, when you provided the Marketing Lens Diagnostic Report™ I knew you were the right company. Your assessment of why I was not attracting the customers I wanted was spot on. You also showed me what I need to focus on to attract the customers I deserve.

Entrepreneur.com's endorsement of Marketing Lens Diagnosis and Growth Program™ was also key to my decision to check you out. They are a trusted resource with information for every business owner.

Still, even at this stage I felt marketing was too complicated for me. Besides, I truly love performing accounting services, *not* marketing my business. Finally, after having followed the Action Plan on Social Media, I was ready to buy the Marketing Lens Growth Program™. I understand now that things are not as complicated as they seemed, and that even I can attract and engage online with potential clients for my firm!

I couldn't wait to get going, so as soon as I could, I performed the Marketing Lens Diagnosis™. I quickly started with the first action on Educational Marketing Tactic™, which made me feel comfortable that I'd made the right decision. I see how, by the end of the Growth Program, I will have become a marketing guru for my business; customers will come to us, as bees are attracted to a honeypot. And you know what? I now see myself as *managing an accounting practice*, and no longer as doing accounting services. The latter is the job of my employees!

Want to grow your business and don't know how and where to start? Or do you have a business challenge you want an expert opinion on?

I love bringing new ideas to the table and contributing to the growth of any kind of business, from e-commerce sites to professional service providers; from retail to entertainment. Every industry has its own particularities, but all have one thing in common: apply best business practices and your business will succeed. It's exactly this subject that I've mastered, and I can help any business implement best practices, regardless of size, industry or geography.

So contact me via my website and I'll respond within 24 hours.

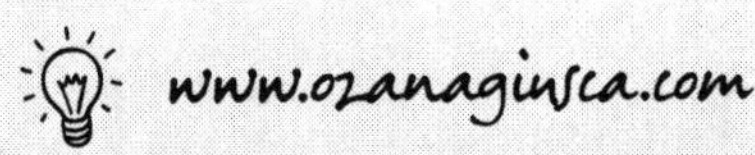

If you just want to stay in touch, connect with me on:

https://plus.google.com/+OzanaGiusca

www.facebook.com/ozana.giusca

http://www.linkedin.com/in/ozanagiusca

https://twitter.com/OzanaGiusca

http://klout.com/OzanaGiusca

Glossary of Terms

These definitions are crafted to be as simple as possible, and are explained in the context of this book.

AAA rating - refers to the evaluation of credit worthiness; i.e how trustworthy a company is to do business with. The highest rating is AAA, descending to C (low) and D (even worse).

Action Plan - a step-by-step guide to work on and improve various areas of the business (strategy, sales, marketing, etc.) and sub-areas (educational marketing, writing blogs, building a website, email marketing etc.).

Affiliate Marketing - this is an agreement whereby a business rewards someone (affiliate person or company) for each visitor / customer brought by the affiliate's own marketing efforts, or for each purchase generated by the affiliate, within a time frame.

Attractive Premium - an item included in a pack, together with less interesting items, and sold as a bundle. It's a good way of moving slow-selling products.

Automate / Automating / Automation - using software rather than employees to undertake automatically some processes within the company.

Business-to-business (B2B) - a business that sells to another businesses. Compare with Business-to-Consumer (B2C), which is when the company sells to consumers / individuals.

Better Offer - a product (service) or a bundle of products (services), designed to offer more value (than usual) for the same dollar spent.

Brand - the name, design, symbol, colors or any other feature that identifies one company or product. For example, Coca-Cola is one brand, Fanta is another; they both belong to The Coca-Cola Company.

Branding via Association - linking the brand of one business with a better known brand, so the lesser known brand 'borrows' from the popularity of the other.

Business Doctor - business growth solution consisting of (i) diagnosing a business (see Business Lens), (ii) designing a customized action plan to optimize and grow the company and (iii) implementing that plan.

Business Lens® - company assessment toolkit to show business owners the naked truth about their company. It identifies unexploited growth potential. It covers everything that matters for the growth of the business (analyzes in detail 15 business dimensions, including Strategy, Innovation, Leadership, Superstar Organization, Marketing, Sales, Human Resources, Motivation, Support Systems, Follow-Up and Organizational Culture).

Business Lens® Diagnostic - the process of answering multiple choice questions and getting a business evaluation report that shows what the business does well and what it needs to focus on.

Buying Criteria - the requirements and rules that one buyer uses to buy a product, such as quality, price, availability, reliability, durability, comfort, habit, safety, freshness, coolness, taste, production methods, etc.

Chunking - grouping together information into ideally sized pieces, so they can be used effectively to produce the outcome one wants without stress or shutdown.

Chunk Down - dealing with smaller parts of information / activities in order to understand or do them effectively. It is especially useful when the information / activities are new or complex.

Chunk Up - dealing with larger parts of information / activities in order to understand / accomplish more at once. Especially useful when one faces known information or deals with routine activities

Complementary Product (Service) - product (service) whose use is interrelated with the use of another product (service). E.g. cartridges and printers are complementary products.

Cross Selling - one business selling its product (service) to another business's customers, and vice versa.

Distribution Channel - the path through which products travel from vendors to consumers. E.g. coffee travels from farmer to exporter, to importer, to distributor, and to the retailer who sells to the end user.

Educational Marketing - sharing valuable information with potential customers, for their benefit and to build trust.

Gift with Purchase - providing another product (service) when someone buys a certain product (service). E.g. a sample cream when you buy a perfume.

Host-parasite Relationship - adding one's product to be sold passively together with another product that is marketed and sold by the other business. (the 'parasite' company doesn't do anything to make sales happen). E.g. producer of a dress adds belt from another manufacturer, and promotes and sells the dress with the belt.

Inducement(s) - an incentive to make the offering more appealing to the customer, and the sale sweeter.

Joined Offers - offering one's product together with another product; both parties promote the combined offer.

Joint Venture (JV) - business agreement for a set period, in which each party undertakes some efforts, for the benefit of all parties.

Lead - term used for a potential customer in the first stage of a sales process; i.e. the business made the initial contact with that prospect, be it (directly or indirectly) via the business's website, or via a phone call or meeting.

Lead Nurturing Email - email designed to build relationships and trust with prospective customers in a consistent and relevant manner.

Limited Edition - the manufacturing of a product in a limited quantity, to make it a more interesting purchase for the buyer.

Limited Time Offer - an offer that has a specific deadline, to give potential buyers a clear reason to act without delay.

Limited Stock Offer - a limited number of items made available, to give potential buyers a clear reason to act without delay.

Locking Sales In - securing long-term sales; e.g. signing a long-term contract or ensuring customer comes back for repeat purchase.

Offer Email - an email to promote a product, to ask for a purchase.

Potentials or Prospects - potential customers.

Pre-emptive Anti-competition Strategy - a strategy employed by one business to lead potentials to only consider its offering, thus blocking its competitors even before they are considered by the buyer as potential sellers.

Risk Reversal - marketing strategy based on removing the risks of the buyer to help them make the purchase decision; e.g. 30-day money back guarantee.

ROI (Return on Investment) - a performance measure calculated as the benefit produced by an investment divided by the cost of that investment

(expressed as %); commonly used to evaluate the efficiency of an investment or to compare different real or potential investments.

ROTI (Return on Time Invested) - the return on the time invested into an activity or project (valued in dollar amount per hour).

Sales Funnel - a metaphoric description of the sales process from initial contact to final sale. It is called a 'funnel', because there are many leads (cold potentials), and as one gets closer to the sale, the number decreases.

Soft Skills - a cluster of personality traits, social abilities, communication, language, and personal habits that characterize relationships of one person with others.

Tooliers® - online platform with business growth tools designed to help small and mid-sized business owners to take their companies to the next level.

Ultimate Strategic Position (USP) (not to be confused with Unique Selling Proposition) – the final perception that a company wants to have in the eyes of the customer.

Unique Selling Proposition (UVP) - a few words used by one business to tell prospective customers why they should buy their product or use their service; it tells how this business adds more value or better solves a problem than competing businesses (similar to Unique Selling Proposition).

Value Papers - promotional materials (such as flyers, leaflets, brochures, catalogues) that give, besides the usual information / advertising content, monetary value to the holder towards the purchase of the product / service being promoted (such as % discount, $ reduction, gift); the goal is to incentivize a sale.

'Any ending is a new beginning.'
Ozana Giusca

Make the most of the knowledge you have received or gotten from this book and take your business to the next level.

Made in the USA
Middletown, DE
29 December 2016